In Search of Nell

B.G. Musick

**Jan-Carol
Publishing, Inc**
"every story needs a book"

In Search of Nell
B.G. Musick

Published July 2017
Little Creek Books
Imprint of Jan-Carol Publishing, Inc
Copyright © 2017 by B.G. Musick
Cover photograph by April Tarjick

ISBN: 978-1-945619-32-8
Library of Congress Control Number: 2017951025

You may contact the publisher:
Jan-Carol Publishing, Inc
PO Box 701
Johnson City, TN 37605
publisher@jancarolpublishing.com
jancarolpublishing.com

This book is dedicated to victims of domestic violence.

AUTHOR'S NOTE

This book is a work of creative nonfiction. It is the true story of my life growing up in a small town in the mountains of Southwest Virginia. Through the genre of creative nonfiction, I was able to utilize my memories, my personal experiences and observations, my subjective perceptions, and my personal points of view. Although there may be others whose perceptions do not parallel mine, these are *my* memories to share. Some names have been altered to protect the privacy of certain individuals.

ACKNOWLEDGMENTS

Steve Chase—Although I owe many thanks to my dear friends and family members for encouraging me to finish this book, I would especially like to thank my husband, Steve, who helped me in more ways than he realized. Writing is cathartic…and it was difficult during the early years of writing about my personal journey. Thank you for supporting my endeavors during the tough chapters. In Connie May Fowler's words, you "helped me face my ghosts."

Peggy Cheney—Thank you, Peggy, for your patience and assistance in the editing of this book.

Dr. Amy Clark—Many thanks to you, Amy, for agreeing to critique my early chapters and encouraging me to publish my story. Dr. Clark is the co-author of *Talking Appalachian: Voice, Identity, and Community.*

Reatha Linkenhoker—Thank you, Aunt Reatha, for your encouraging words and help during the writing process.

Vanessa Murphy—Many thanks to my daughter, Vanessa, for believing in me throughout this process. It was your love of the old stories that inspired me to put them down in writing. All my love to our sweet Jared and Jayce.

Helen Owens—Many thanks to you, Helen, for the hours of long distance phone calls to help me edit the book; I could not have done it without you. Our week together in "The Sinks" will be forever implanted in my mind as a special time. Helen is a friend and a former co-worker from Honaker High School, as well as my former high school English teacher at Cleveland High School. She is the author of a historical novel, *Stand and Face the Morning*.

Vern Powers—Much thanks and appreciation for allowing me to use your home in "The Sinks" to edit this book.

Devon Price—Many thanks to my son, Devon, for his patience in waiting for this book to be finished. All my love to our sweet Kaela and Kyle.

PROLOGUE

This story is engraved into Mercy's heart. She can quote it by rote—chapter and verse. As far back as she can remember, the voices have echoed in her ears. She would sit quietly in the shadows of the room or on the edge of the porch with her legs dangling down ready to flee if the adults realized she was present. She listened (while pretending not to do so) to them re-tell the story of her birth.

In the tattered front seat of his Uncle Taze's old 1940 pickup truck, R.C. dawdled cautiously around the meandering, horseshoe-shaped curves on Cleveland Mountain. He had already traveled five miles from his home in Back Valley and passed through the small town of Cleveland, VA. He listened to each groan and click of the truck's engine as he shifted gears, climbing toward the crest of the hill. He was well aware the town of Lebanon, VA was still seven miles away, that it was well past midnight, and that his wife, Nell, was in the latter stages of giving birth to their third child. R.C. was unable to afford his own vehicle, so the truck was on loan for this unexpected trip. As he turned the bend near the crest of the mountain, he was certain he could not make it on time to Lebanon General Hospital.

Nell had already lost control of her bowels. There was no other choice, no time for modesty. Blood seeped bit by bit onto the seat, permeating the cracks and seams and onto the floorboard.

She screamed, "Git on with it, I can't wait! I can't wait!" And she proceeded to give birth, right there in Uncle Taze's old pickup truck.

Unable to halt the contractions and the natural order of things, Nell positioned her weary body against the door, pushed with all her strength and brought forth new life. In its eagerness to be born, the baby simply gushed forth and followed the trail of blood. With the umbilical cord still wrapped dangerously around its neck, the newborn plopped with a dull thud onto the floorboard.

"Oh m' God, Oh m' God, git it up! Git it up!" R.C. yelled as he reached toward the baby. The muscles of his right arm tightened. Determined his baby wouldn't die on the floorboard of a truck before he reached the hospital, he nudged Nell into a forward position and helped her gather up their newborn. Coming back to the task at hand, his neck and hand wrenched to the left. Like a night bird navigating unfamiliar territory, his eyes squinted, his pupils dilated and a sense of purpose propelled him forward into the cold October night at breakneck speed—toward the hospital and toward help.

The baby mewled… then again, and again. Nell stretched forward, untangled the umbilical cord and lifted the newborn into her arms. It was a girl, their first, and she didn't appear to be concerned about the dramatic events of her birth.

R.C. heard the cry.

I ain't got no time to look. No time to check the toes and fingers. Sounds jist like the other kids when they was born.

With each high-pitched cry, R.C. was thankful his first daughter had survived, at least for now.

She's a tuff'n, she'll be a survivor, I jist know it, but how's Uncle Taze gonna feel about his truck bein' such a mess? I reckon the baby don't seem to mind though. Lissen', she's jist a-wailin' away!

Reinforcing his hands on the steering wheel, R.C. resumed his

2

concentration on the mountain road, on his newborn baby, and on his wife, Nell.

As if in a catatonic stupor, Nell sat silently. No comment. She stared at the new baby and silently counted the fingers and toes.

They're all there. No birthmark. Thas good but jist look at this other lil' mouth to feed. What am I gonna do?

By the time they reached Slab Town, R. C. and Nell were hearing whimpers only every now and then. Their greatest fear was that the baby wouldn't survive. They hadn't cut the cord. So with mother and baby still attached, the old truck picked up speed and lurched forward through the town square, past the Confederate Monument, the funeral home and the Methodist Church, and into the empty parking lot.

Leaping from the truck, R.C. yelled, "Help me! Help me! My wife's had a baby!" Hovering outside the truck, he could provide no further help. He felt helpless.

Well, I reckon I done the best I could. Oh, Lord, please let 'em both live.

From the open door, a nurse yelled, "Well, bring her on in! Quick!"

"No, you don't understan, she's already had it!" R. C. fumed, unable to conceal the frustration and fear in his voice. "Couldn't somebody jist please hurry!"

Nurses swarmed to the parked truck and affirmed mother and baby were still attached. Helping them both onto a stretcher, they rushed them inside and cut the umbilical cord.

Mercella Gail snuggled into her mother's arms and suckled her mother's breast for the first time. She would be called Mercy.

The year was 1952 and her life's journey was just beginning. Her birth was like an omen that, as time passed, would return to haunt her again and again.

"Opportunity"
Ella Wheeler Wilcox

Send forth your heart's desire, and work and wait;
The opportunities of life are brought
To our own doors, not by capricious fate,
But by the strong compelling force of thought.

CHAPTER 1

NELL

Later, while lying in the hospital bed, Nell thought about her life and why she'd let herself become pregnant—again.

I jist can't figger it out! I'm jist nineteen, this bein' my third child and all, I can't let this happen again! Besides, we can't afford 'nother mouth to feed with the two boys already. R.C. with no job and everythin', hit's a hard row to hoe. I'll jist have to be more careful the next time R.C. comes home a-drinkin'.

Yet somehow, she felt blessed. Her first child, Darrell, had been born at the Musick family home when she was just 16. R.C.'s mother, a midwife, helped to birth the baby. Her second child, Gary Wayne, had also been born at home.

"It sure feels good to be in this here hospital," she mumbled as her eyes closed. Waves of delicate pink clouds enveloped her as sleep took over her weary body. Visions of newborn babies haunted her dreams throughout the night. All placed in tidy rows, each baby screamed to be fed as tiny arms reached out toward her. Hours later, Nell woke drenched in sweat and with newfound dread.

'Nother baby for me to take home. What in God's name will we all do?

Her small-framed body shook as she gave way to tears—alone. Nell knew exactly how hard her life was already, and that people often made snide remarks like "Boy, she's sure a high-spirited woman, a lil' briggety, too." Nell just *hmphed* at their comments.

Nell was a pretty woman. Her medium-length, curly hair boasted a slight hint of copper, the red especially noticeable from a distance in the afternoon sun. Only five feet four inches tall, she was a petite woman and her feisty personality was plain to see, even to the most casual eye.

R.C. drove home to Back Valley, cleaned the blood from his Uncle Taze's truck as best he could, and within a few days moved to Detroit City.

I've already got three lil' uns! I've had enough of barely scrapin' by. Besides, I'm a worldly man. Why, I've even been in the U.S. Army. I've had lots of experience drivin' them Army officers 'round the Philippines. It's time for me to leave these mountains, leave Back Valley, jist leave it all behind! I got bigger-n-better plans for my family. Jist leave the kids at home; no place to raise a family in the city. I'll jist send money back home to Nell and the kids.

Family and neighbors often said, "That R.C., he's a looker, and quite a catch for some young woman." His raven hair and his family's deep-set brown eyes still caught the ladies' attention, even long after he had married Nell. Standing nearly six feet tall with a slender build, he had a smile that had melted the hearts of many women in the mountains. Before leaving for the army, he had courted a number of eligible young ladies. And after his return from WWII at the age of 21, he had an air about him that made him even more desirable. Since not many eligible bachelors left the mountains and returned, being an experienced, mature, Army man only added to the qualities that made him attractive. But he had found Nell's personality charming. She had a loud, hearty laugh he had found irresistible. Although he was seven years older, he wooed her, loved her, and when she was with child, married her.

Detroit (pronounced "Dee-troit") City was the "land of milk and honey," according to people in the mountains. In 1952, work was scarce and people abandoned the Appalachians in droves. Migrating to the North in search of a better life, they fled from every hollow throughout Southwestern Virginia, including Russell County. Hard working people, they settled into jobs at Ford Motor Company, General Motors, and Chrysler, glad to get any job that would pay a better wage than the $3 a day offered back home on the tobacco farms.

Within a few months, R.C. had lost his taste for life in the city. Not what he'd expected, the glamour of city life melted away. When questioned about living in Detroit, he would scoff and say, "It's got too much traffic, too much exhaust from them cars, too many people, and not enough home-cooked vittles, like soup beans and corn bread. Why, you can't even buy a decent piece o' corn bread in Dee-troit."

I dreaded wakin' up ever day up North. I hated them Yankees callin' me a hillbilly and mockin' my speech. Damn them Yankees! They can have the flat land!

So, like many others before him, R.C. returned to the comfort of the mountains, eager to join Nell, Darrell, Gary Wayne, and baby Mercy. In time, he found a job driving a truck, hauling slate for a local coal company.

I don't reckon I'm to blame for the hard times we've seen. I provided a home for Nell and the kids. She's jist never been satisfied! I know we spent the first few months livin' with my folks, but we have our own place now. Why, it's even near kinfolk, so Nell can have somebody to visit durin' the day while I'm off at work.

While R.C. was away, Nell enjoyed their tiny two-bedroom home that sat perched on the side of a hill, tucked into a small valley near Weaver's Creek Baptist Church and directly across from Uncle Taze's house. She loved living there and took their youngest child, Mercy, to visit Uncle Taze and Aunt Lucy over and over again. Nell liked to talk to them about how much Mercy was growing.

After all, the baby seen her first breath of life in Uncle Taze's ole pickup truck. It only seems right to honor 'im in some way.

Nell knew Uncle Taze and Aunt Lucy had become attached to the baby, carrying her to Weaver's Creek Baptist Church on Sundays. They'd croon, "We jist wanna show her off to the congregation," and lift her in the air for everyone to view.

I know Lucy longs for a child to call her own. I don't know why all women can't be as fertile as I am.

Lucy begged, "Please let the baby come and stay with us awhile. You know, we'd love to have her fer good." And so, Nell, busy with the other two children, allowed Mercy to stay with them for weeks at a time. She mused on the idea of giving her new baby to Taze and Lucy.

After all, Uncle Taze and Aunt Lucy can give the baby a better home than we can. In their own rights, they have more money, more love, and more time to give. I reckon it would be okay to jist give her to 'em.

Nell, unable to reach a decision concerning the future of her child, simply waited for fate to decide her destiny. And as expected, it eventually did. In the end, the decision would not be hers to make. Aunt Lucy died from cancer when Mercy was nine months old. They buried Aunt Lucy across the road from Nell's home, in clear view of Uncle Taze's front porch, right out beside the old church steps. Mercy was restless, colicky, and fretful for days.

Weeks later, Nell stood on her front porch, which overlooked the nearby hills. She gazed in the direction of the late afternoon sun as it traveled across the sky. Like an owl hunting its prey, Nell's eyes searched for that little plot of land. She sensed the familiar ripples rolling from the pit of her stomach. Ignoring them, she lifted her gaze, her eyes darting past the old chestnut tree and the apple orchard, and squinted as she focused on Lucy's grave. Her hands shifted to loosen the buttons on her washed-out flannel shirt. Her fingers caressed the outlines of her gut.

"That cancer done eat her clean up." Nell mumbled to no one in particular.

A few months later, Nell gave birth to her second daughter, Joyce, her fourth child. By this time, she was 21 years old.

The next time R.C. comes home a-drinkin', I'm gonna have to be more careful!

Nell cried—again.

The following year, R.C. and Nell settled into a new home on Sandy Ridge. It was more isolated than Weaver's Creek, more out-of-the-way than their previous home, with no running water. But there was still some flat land, and Clinchfield Coal Company had not yet bought out all of the older homes.

Nell said, "Hit's a new start for our family, and near my family's old home place this time. Hit'll be a good change for us."

Within a few months, Lynn was born. Nell cried—again.

I vow to be plumb ill with R.C. the next time he comes home a-drinkin'. And I swanee, I mean it this time!

Shortly after Lynn's birth, the three-room house burned to the ground mysteriously in the middle of the night. The neighbors had witnessed the house burning. In the distance across the mountains, they had seen the blaze light up the night sky and screamed, "Oh, Lord A-mercy, Nell, your house is on fire!"

Nell sprinted to the neighbor's front porch and stood in disbelief as the yellow flames spewed across Sourwood Mountain.

Well, he's done it this time. He's really done it. He's tried to kill me...and the childern!

The following day, Nell stood alone gazing at her family's old homestead, all while her stomach churned and flopped. Mixed with the acid leftovers from a rushed morning meal, the food settled uncomfortably in her gut and then forced itself back into her throat, leaving a soured taste in her mouth. In a daze, she thought about the fire that could've killed her...and all the children.

R.C.'s mean when he's been a-drinkin'. Came home yesterday afternoon and beat me with that belt—again.

Absentmindedly, her hand moved down to touch the tenderness on her right hip; it throbbed painfully. But the physical pain was much less troubling than the grief she felt in her heart.

Afterward, she had fled to the closest neighbors with her children late in the night. Nell had been afraid of her husband and his liquored-up temper. But most of all, she dreaded his thrashings with that belt. Over time, the beatings had become harsher.

God help me! What'll I do?

Lost in her trance-like thoughts, Nell had not seen R.C. approach—but she *heard* him. She caught sight of R.C. in the shadows, near where the house had once stood. She braced herself for the coming confrontation.

Without hesitating, Nell yelled at R.C. "You're always smokin' in that bed! I jist *know* thas how it started!"

A more sobered R.C. shot back, "I can't be blamed for that! I know I wasn't smokin' in bed! Besides, all five kids are all right; nobody's hurt, and we're downright lucky."

And that was the end of the argument. Nell knew she would be beaten again if she kept on accusing R.C.

Only the banty doodies in the cage beside the house had died.

I sure feel rotten when the lil' uns ask me 'bout them banty chicks. Sad to see them lil' things all shriveled and burnt up like that.

Truth be told, it was just a guess on Nell's part that R.C. had deliberately burned down their home. She never really knew.

The family's next move was a short distance from the old burned-out home. This time it was a weathered clapboard house, its weight supported in back by stilts 20 feet high. The front porch overlooked the main road; more importantly, it offered Nell a chance to visit with neighbors.

"I'm sure pleased to have somebody near us," Nell said quietly as she looked at R.C. "And the front yard, it's all level! The kids'll have a chance to romp n' play without me havin' to be there."

"Yeah. Thas good, ain't it?"

I know I done my best this time; I know it don't have runnin' water, but neither did our first house. Nell will jist have to walk the quarter mile back to the old burned-out house to fetch water from the well. Besides, she's used to pumpin' water and makin' it last.

Reminding her of their last disaster with fire, R.C. warned

time and again, "Don't leave them young 'uns in the house alone with fire in that pot-bellied stove!" And off he would leave for work on the tunnel through Wilder Mountain.

Good payin' work for me at last. Thank the Lord!

But R.C. and Nell could not know that hard times and another disaster were ready to befall their family again.

CHAPTER 2

ANOTHER FIRE ON SANDY RIDGE

From a distance, Mercy heard the shrill voices of her neighbors screaming time and again, from somewhere near the main road. Unable to make sense of all the chaos, she became confused. Sensing the urgency in the screams, Mercy scurried from the bedroom, sprinted past the living room, and stumbled through the front door into the cold night air. Mercy paused for a brief moment, just long enough to determine the cause of the commotion. Her house was on fire!

As she stood outside in the snow, adults questioned her—but she couldn't seem to understand. She just remembered seeing the orange and yellow flames rolling across the ceiling. Adults kept screaming, "Whur's Nell? Whur's the other young'uns?" The by-standers closed in around Mercy, but all she remembered later was how cold it was standing there in the snow—without shoes.

Down the road, Nell busied herself with the daily chore of filling water buckets from the old well pump. As she turned homeward with her heavy load, the wind shifted, forcing the smell of smoke deep into her nostrils. Glancing upward, she saw the blazing flames in the distance. Tossing the water buckets, she raced at top speed toward home. *Oh, no, not again!* As she dashed around the curve, she witnessed the tragedy unfolding. Time stood still.

Stop, breathe. The childern... Count 'em; one, two, three, fo', fi'— Whur's Lynn? Whur's Joyce?!

From deep in her throat, a guttural scream escaped. "Can't y'all *hear* me? Whur's Lynn? Find Lynn! Find Joyce!"

Neighbors had alerted the older children, but had forgotten the newest additions to the family—the new baby and two-year-old Joyce. Lynn had been sleeping peacefully in her crib in the back bedroom, and Nell knew there was little time to take action. Without pause, she jumped through the glass windowpanes in a side room and lunged toward the back bedroom. She felt the scorching heat from the flames that circled the walls and licked at the sides of the crib. Nell saw Joyce trying to lift Lynn from her crib, to no avail. Grabbing Joyce, Nell threw her as far away from the flames as possible—right out the side window and onto the ground. Finally, Nell reached Lynn, hastily plucked her from the blankets, and threw her from the open window—then jumped through behind her. It was a risk, she knew, but both children survived.

Thank God. Jist one lil' scratch on Lynn's arm from a nail left hangin' on the side of the old house. And a burn on one arm. Both childern will be all right. I reckon we been lucky again.

On his way home from work, R.C. saw the blaze just as the car rounded the last stiff curve. The horseshoe bend, one of the most feared on the mountain, was situated high above the surrounding hills. It provided a glimpse of his little home through the woods. His worst fears had been realized: Another home on fire!

"Oh, m'God, whur's the young'uns?"

They had lived in the house for less than a year, and lost everything *again*. Everything, that is, except the lives of their children. They had recently bought Christmas presents for everyone, which included flannel shirts, britches, underwear, and winter coats for all the kids.

"We're survivors," Nell told everyone.

"Survivin' in the mountains is tough for everybody, we ain't no different," R.C. said. They had endured in the past; they would prevail again.

Within a few weeks, their new trailer was hauled up the mountain by an old Jeep and placed on a flat piece of land at the top of Sandy Ridge, near the site where their first home had burned. It was the perfect place to have a home—and rightfully so, Nell proclaimed. It had a level yard, a scarcity on Sourwood Mountain.

Pride welled up inside Nell when she saw her trailer all situated for the first time. Her newly-fenced front yard looked out upon the crossroads where the four roads going up or down the mountain intersected. The five children had more than enough room to play in the nearby apple orchard, romping with their collie and playing hide-n-seek in the barn. The trailer had no running water, so Nell used the old well pump in the side yard and the run-down outhouse just a short walk from the front door. She told herself she was more than satisfied.

Mercy blossomed as she explored the mountains. She and her brothers, along with the Wilson kids down the hill, spent hours pushing and riding coal cars in and out…in and out…in and out of the abandoned coal mine.

Of course, mommy and daddy didn't know, or I reckon we'd all get a right good whuppin'.

Luckily, her mother was kept busy during the day with the two younger children. By now, Mercy had a new baby brother, Randy. She remembered how her mother cried the day she'd brought him home from the hospital, but she couldn't understand why.

I'm gonna be plumb ill with R.C. the next time he comes home a-drinkin'. I swanee I am! I really am this time! Nell thought.

Mercy perfected the art of making mud pies, building moss-covered floors for tree houses, and romping through the open fields. She had few worries—except when her parents had an argument. She remembered the last time that had happened, and she tried not to think about it.

But Nell remembered every detail. She recalled clearly another night she almost lost her six children—again.

CHAPTER 3

SOURWOOD MOUNTAIN

In the winter of 1957, torrential rains came once again to the mountains in Southwest Virginia. Hollows, gushing springs, creek beds, and bottoms quickly filled with the runoff. In downtown Cleveland, a palpable fear gripped the town folks as they watched flood waters crest above twenty-four feet. Businesses, roads, homes, and farms were flooded with silt, mud, sand, and debris. Raging waters flooded across the Clinch River bridge in the center of town and transportation to and from rural areas became impossible. It was one of the worst floods in Cleveland's history.

On Sourwood Mountain, the children were forced inside to play. One afternoon, R.C. had come home drinking and his temper overtook him. Nell knew she would not be safe that night. A confrontation took place between them, and he struck her—again. She gathered the older children, hollered, "Foller me!" and carried the babies in her arms. Nell loaded them inside the old Ford coupe and headed toward the home of Lacy Stevens, owner of a grocery store on Sandy Ridge.

We'll jist hide out in that little room behind the store and be safe for the night. I'll make plans to come back in the mornin' and leave R.C.—for good this time. I mean it!

It was hard for Nell to recognize familiar sights in the blinding rain that night, especially without her glasses. They had been broken during the fight, and because of her nearsightedness, it was impossible for her to have a clear view of the narrow, winding road.

Please let me see! Please let me see! R.C.'s really mad at me this time!

The daily torrential rains had caused mudslides in the washboard road. As the Ford Coupe slid around each mountain curve, Nell realized the danger she had placed her children in—but it was too late. When she took her eyes off the road to glance in the rearview mirror, the car slammed into a tree. The tree miraculously held firm. "Thank God," she breathed; her family was saved from the 200-foot drop over the cliff and down the side of Sourwood Mountain.

Inside the car, all the children screamed in unison. Mercy turned toward approaching car lights. Her father's truck had chased closely behind them, and she feared for her mother's safety. She remembered how her father had struck her mother's face more than once in the past.

Oh, don't let 'em quarrel again. Please, don't let 'em quarrel!

There seemed to be no escape for Nell, not with the car lodged against the tree. From the corner of her eye, Nell glimpsed movement and saw R.C. behind her. She dragged the children from the car toward the nearest trees. Nell knew she might not survive R.C.'s wrath, as drunk as he was. Finding refuge under a rocky overhang, she placed Mercy and the others way back, tight against the cliff, to protect them from the onslaught of the pouring rain. Ordering them to remain still until she returned, Nell carried the two babies and ran blindly into the night.

Mercy wept violent tears. The others whimpered softly. Too afraid to cry out or make sudden movements, they didn't dare leave the safety of the cliff. From time to time, bolts of lightning gave them a chance to observe their surroundings. The terrified children watched as tree branches splintered, oak and chestnut leaves blowing past their heads. As sounds of the forest echoed all around, panic overtook them. Mercy huddled with the others, shrinking into herself.

What if she don't come back for us? Whur'd she go? Which way? How will mommy find her way in the dark, carryin' the young'uns?

She warned her younger sister to stop sniveling. They all waited, unsure what would happen if their daddy discovered them first. For Mercy, the night passed at a snail's pace. With each movement of the relentless wind and each critter's sound in the woods, the muscles in her tiny body stiffened even more. Her hair stood on end. She hugged her brothers, shushed Joyce and stolidly waited for her mother.

I gotta be a big girl now. Gotta be brave. Gotta be brave.

Minutes passed, maybe even hours. Mercy couldn't tell how much time had actually gone by; the innocence of childhood sheltered her from such knowledge. Seconds, minutes, hours, and infinity had no meaning in her short life.

Time dragged on, but suddenly a faint sound came through the dripping forest. Alert now and with all senses heightened, Mercy tilted her head toward the sound. It stopped briefly, moved forward; it paused again. Someone moved toward the cliff, yelled, then moved forward again. At the next streak of lightning, Mercy caught a glimpse of her mother's face. *She came back!* Mercy scrambled past the others, rose from beneath the cliff to grab her mother's hand, and tumbled into her arms. The other children, by now aroused from their stupor, scrambled out to greet their mother.

They all reached safety that night; friends provided them a safe haven. Mercy didn't know their names. She was simply thankful to have the dry clothes and soft bed provided them for the night.

Nell thought about leaving R.C. that night. In the past, she knew she had always appeased him by returning home each time she had left him. He had always begged, pleaded, and made promises.

Oh, what should I do? What can *I do? For the love of my children, maybe I should give it one more try to keep our family together. Besides, whur can I go with six childern? Who'd help us? Who'd give us money? Who'd feed the childern, clothe 'em? Mandy owns a hotel in downtown Bluefield. I could go there for a while. There'd be plenty o' empty rooms left. Josie lives there too, and she promised to help us. But R.C. always comes high-tailin' it after me, though. Always sweet talks me into comin' home again. I love 'im, so maybe I'll try again. In spite of his drinkin', he is a hard workin' man. I married him, and I guess I'll try one more time to keep our family together.*

And so, with her six children, she returned to the little trailer she loved so dearly on Sourwood Mountain.

CHAPTER 4

SCHOOLHOUSE ON SOURWOOD MOUNTAIN

By fall, Mercy was overjoyed about the preparations for school.

I'm ready to learn some readin' an writin'. Why, I can already spell my name, cuz Darrell teached me.

By now, Darrell was in third grade. As her oldest brother, he had been cruel to her on a regular basis. Mercy remembered the day he'd forced her to eat coffee grounds from the trailer floor for no good reason. Her mother often left him in charge of all the others, and Mercy held a grudge against her brother.

I reckon he jist wants to be the man in charge o' things, so I ate them coffee grounds, licked 'em right up off that floor. In spite of him bein' so mean, I do 'preciate his helpin' me print my name.

The faded, one-room schoolhouse on Sourwood Mountain was a short distance from Mercy's house: Straight across the gravel road, down one gently sloping hill, up another, and around a couple of bends. Only one mile from the main crossroads on Sandy Ridge, it was an easy trek to and from school. It was child's play for mountain kids already in good shape and young enough to carry out the task with little effort.

In Mercy's mind, the schoolhouse was a wondrous sight. It was unlike anything she had ever seen before, with its coatroom, oversized windowpanes, and potbellied stove in the middle of the large classroom. School began in early fall. The trees had not yet begun to change colors, but the cool mornings and night air hinted at an early arrival of the change in seasons. Proudly wearing her sister's new coat, Mercy bundled up for her first day of school. She wanted to escape the boredom of being left at home with the smaller children and was ready to spell her name on the big blackboard. She did—and it was *wrong*!

Mr. George Barton, her teacher, insisted it was misspelled.

"No, Mercy. You've written your name wrong on the board. Try it again."

"Whut's the difference? It don't make no matter…and my brother is stupid!" she argued with him.

So, she continued printing "MERCI" every single day on her papers until Mr. Barton decided to punish her by forcing her to print it correctly on that big blackboard in front of all the other students. Over and over again…and over again…500 times. By then, Mercy felt certain she'd learned the proper way to spell her name. In the beginning, she had stubbornly refused to cooperate with her teacher, continuing to spell it wrong—even on the blackboard. By the end of the week, Mr. Barton had won his battle with

Mercy. But she wasn't the least bit happy about it, and tucked this early lesson about teachers into the back of her mind. *Don't cross your teacher, especially your very first one!*

In the one-room schoolhouse there were six rows of students, with four to five students in each row. Each grade had its own row of seats. Mercy was in the first grade, so she sat in the first row. Second grade, second row, and so on across the room.

I can't believe them sixth graders are so big, all the way over there in that sixth-grade row.

Each day Nell packed three lunches—one for Darrell, one for Gary Wayne, and one for her daughter, Mercy. Inside, she put corn bread, soup beans, and sometimes a biscuit or two. More often than not, nothing was inside the biscuit.

Life's hard, and I don't have extras to put in them lunches. I do the best I can to feed 'em ever day. Them round, aluminum coal minin' buckets sure do come in handy for packin' lunches for the young'uns.

Each morning, Mercy was careful when carrying her food to school. Balancing her feast for the midday dinner, she kept one hand on the lunch pail and another on the Mason jar she carried. Since the schoolhouse did not have running water, each child was responsible for bringing water to school. Each day, Mercy carried a Mason jar filled with water from the nearby spring. She had quickly learned that water was a precious commodity.

Mercy loved school because she enjoyed learning better than anything else. Like all the other girls on the mountain, she played house during recess. They gathered smooth rocks and soft fern mosses from the nearby forests for carpeting their playhouse floors. Hopscotch and hide-n-seek were popular games with both boys and girls, but Mercy noticed most of the older boys liked playing hide-n-seek with the older girls.

I jist don't know why.

One morning, Mercy couldn't find her new white, cotton panties to wear to school. She couldn't imagine going to school and playing house in the woods that day without her white cotton go-to-school panties. She searched relentlessly through the house, then searched again.

What'll I do? I don't reckon Mr. Barton would 'preciate me not wearin' bloomers. Whur in the world? Mommy's always warshin' clothes out under that tree in the back yard. I jist know they oughta be around here somewhur.

Even in the coldest days of winter, the clothesline was always full of clothes trying to dry. Having checked the clothesline with no luck, Mercy decided to steal Joyce's frilly panties, the ones with the little rows of lace decorating the backs. They were a little snug and embarrassing for her to wear, and she felt a little stab of guilt when she put them on.

I jist really hope ole Joyce don't find out. But at least I won't have to stay home and miss any learnin'.

And off down the road she skipped to school. She was a happy child and couldn't imagine the time she'd be forced to ride the big yellow school bus down that mountain road, traveling 20 miles away to the Cleveland School. It was a daunting thought for her, and she would rather not think about abandoning the sanctuary she'd found on her mountain.

But this was not to be.

CHAPTER 5

LEFT ALONE

By now, R. C. was working in Eastern Virginia. Nell enjoyed traveling with him from time to time and would leave the children in the care of nearby neighbors on the mountain. But on this particular day, Mercy didn't know where or why her parents had gone. She simply knew she and her brothers and sisters were all alone, for a *long* time. She was uneasy.

But Mommy and Daddy'll be home soon, won't they?

Much to Mercy's dismay, Darrell appeared to be in charge again. She felt a sense of dread at the realization she'd likely fall victim to some strange torment at his hands.

Her baby brother, Randy, was now six months old. She had learned to feed him the bottle when he cried, and had even learned to change diapers. After all, she was five years old—the oldest girl—and considered responsible for her age. Darrell was ill-tempered again and pushed her around, but she stood her ground. Mercy had no memory of eating coffee grounds, at least not this time.

Hunger pains came quickly. She, as well as her siblings, opened the refrigerator more than once in search of food. Cold biscuits garnished with ample amounts of sandwich spread had long since disappeared. Mercy hoped her mommy and daddy would return home before nightfall—but that would not be the case. Sometime during the night, the children had finally been able to fall asleep, bellies empty.

The following day, the older children cared for the younger ones, Randy and Lynn, as best they could. Soon the baby's milk would be gone, and Mercy was worried: a sense of responsibility overwhelmed her. Again, she had no concept of the passing of time. None of them did.

More than once, Mercy warned Joyce not to climb the fence around the front yard. But Joyce ignored the warnings, as usual… and ripped her favorite panties, the ones with the rows of frilly lace on the back end. Joyce cried, then cried some more. But Mercy didn't feel pity for her; she was just disappointed she would never be able to steal them again to wear to school.

Since no adults were around to supervise, Lynn and Joyce fought more than usual. Joyce struck Lynn with a hoe, hit her right across the eyebrow and brought blood. But the children had learned to be tough and resilient. Refusing to be outdone, Lynn had struck Joyce right back with another hoe, right above her eye. Mercy grew tired of refereeing her two younger sisters.

Throughout the following day and night, the fierce mountain wind blew nonstop. The trailer seemed to rock on its foundation, but maybe it was only Mercy's imagination. She'd always been fearful their trailer would be blown over during the night, even when her parents had been there. Fifteen feet from their back yard was a sheer drop off the side of the mountain. All the children had been cautioned about playing near the edge of the yard.

Sleep did not come easily that night. Another day passed, and they finished the last remaining dried crumbs from the sandwich-spread biscuits. Randy's milk had soured, and Mercy could not remember what she had done with his dirty diapers. She thought she had thrown them down the toilet hole in the outhouse. More than once, they scavenged the garden and apple orchard for cucumbers and tiny green apples to eat. Days and nights came and passed in a blur.

Then Uncle Denver and cousin Raleigh (Hawk was his nickname) brought supplies for all of them. Fresh light bread, milk, and bologna had never tasted so good! They filled their stomachs, fed the baby, and reluctantly waved goodbye to their saviors. Before they left, Mercy questioned them about her parents, but they had no news for her.

Whur's my mommy? Whur's my daddy? How long will it be before they git back? Alone again. I reckon I'll never understand grownups! Why'd they leave us? Please come back, please, don't leave us alone!

Again, the six children survived. Mercy never knew how many days the six of them had been left alone to fend for themselves. Most of what happened on Sourwood Mountain grew fuzzy with time, and Mercy was thankful for that; she didn't want to know the truth. Mercy shoved the painful memories of the experience into the darkest recesses of her mind, determined not to recall them for a long time to come. If ever.

Best not to think about them things.

R.C. eventually returned home, but this time without Nell. Within days, the six children were placed in separate homes. Darrell and Gary Wayne moved to Back Valley with R.C.'s parents, Aunt Mattie and Uncle Daff. They were an elderly couple, and could use the boys' help on their small tobacco farm. Darrell was seven and Gary Wayne was six, old enough to slop the hogs, hoe and till the gardens, milk the cows, and help the aging couple. Aunt Mattie had a special place in her heart for Darrell, since she had delivered him into the world. Uncle Daff favored Gary Wayne; he was a quiet child who followed his grandfather's every step on the farm. The two boys would have a solid, stable home with food in their stomachs on a regular basis.

Lynn, by then two years old, went to live with Maynard and Naomi (Omi) in the small town of Cleveland, on the banks of Clinch River. Lynn was a beautiful child. With her curly brown hair, olive skin, and deep-set brown Musick eyes, she projected a beauty far beyond all of the other children. With her big, wide smile and gleeful personality, she quickly charmed everyone around her.

Omi had yearned for a little girl, and she and Maynard were happy to have Lynn join their family of two boys, Bobby Joe and Gerald. Omi, R.C.'s sister, had married Maynard, who was a mandolin player. He promised to play music and sing to Lynn, and teach her to flatfoot. She would enjoy life to the fullest. They made plans to officially adopt her, making her a permanent addition to their family.

"Boy, that Lynn, she's a purty little thing. She's the purtiest one of all them young'uns, ain't she?" Maynard cooed.

"Oh, yeah, she's a darlin' lil' thing," said Omi.

Mercy overheard it all; she couldn't count the number of times she'd heard that comment before. Everyone said it, time and again. "That Lynn's so purty." *So purty…so purty.* The words echoed in her head every time she heard them.

It's like they don't even care if I hear 'em. I feel ugly, unwanted. But at least Lynn will have a good home.

Baby Randy would live with Nell's sister Mildred and her husband, Jim. They lived in downtown Cleveland, not far across the railroad tracks from Lynn. The children would grow up in close proximity to one another, and Aunt Mildred and Uncle Jim seemed happy to have Randy join their three children, Carl, Judy, and Linda. Since Randy was only six months old at the time, he was welcomed into the family by the other children, and they doted on his every whim. A fat, jolly little boy with curly, reddish-brown hair, he quickly settled into the comforts of his new home.

Randy'll have a lovin' home, too.

Mercy never knew why her mother had taken her younger sister, Joyce, away to live with her. She also didn't know where they had moved; it would be years before Mercy had the opportunity to see her sister again.

Why didn't she take me? Probly cuz I ain't as special as Lynn or Joyce.

Mercy's world quickly unraveled. She had no say in the decision of where she would live. For a short period of time, she stayed with Uncle Maynard and Aunt Alma, relatives on her mother's side of the family.

Boy, was I scared of Uncle Maynard, cuz he took his minin' leather strap and gave me a good whuppin' one day. I can't remember what I done, but I know he was purty ill at me!!

Two weeks later, Mercy's mother unexpectedly returned. Excited to see her, Mercy ran and tumbled into her arms, but she soon learned it would be a short visit. Uncle Maynard helped her mother load Mercy's meager belongings into a Piggly Wiggly sack, and placed her in the back seat of the old Jeep for a final trip to Back Valley. Abruptly, they explained to Mercy that she would be living with her grandparents, Mattie and Daff, on the tobacco farm. It was a plan Mercy had not bargained for.

After a short drive, her uncle's old Jeep came to a grinding halt in front of her grandparents' home. Mercy felt a flood of emotions that unforgettable day. She realized her mother was leaving her forever—but she was too young to understand the reasoning behind that decision. She reached for her mother, wrapped her arms around her, and clung to her, but to no avail. Her mother's decision had been made.

Mercy cried and begged, sobbed and pleaded, "Please don't leave me! Please don't leave me!" Her mother lifted her from the Jeep, pushed her toward the gate of her grandparents' home, and simply drove away without her.

This action was beyond Mercy's comprehension. During her five years of life, she had endured an untimely birth, two fires, a near-fatal accident on a mountain road, and had been left abandoned to fend for herself for days—but she was not prepared for this. With a sense of despair beyond all she had ever experienced, she lifted up her tiny sack of clothing, carried it through the lot, walked into the front yard, and halted on the front porch. Sobs wracked her body; she turned to scream for her mother one last time, but it was too late.

Nell disappeared.

CHAPTER 6

ON A TRIAL BASIS

With reluctance and a great sense of loss, Mercy completed first grade at Cleveland Elementary while living with her grandparents. Located on the banks of the Clinch River, this school was larger than the little one on Sourwood Mountain. She was in awe of the six classrooms, gym, nurse's station, and principal's office. Eventually, she learned to enjoy the daily, 10-mile round-trip bus ride to and from Back Valley.

At first, the principal had been reluctant to allow Mercy to attend school. It seemed she had been too young to begin school on Sourwood Mountain. But since she had already begun and apparently done well, the principal conceded. Mercy was grateful; she didn't want to stay home with her grandparents or miss school for even one single day.

Later, her young mind was unable to recall much about the events of that year, but she remembered visiting other relatives for short periods of time. It was always "on a trial basis," she had understood. Her daddy drove her to visit friends and neighbors throughout the mountains, attempting to locate a permanent home for her. Mercy remembered some homes more vividly than others: the old lady in Dickenson County where she had spent a few nights; the two babysitters she had known from before on Sandy Ridge; and Aunt Ida's home, where the foul, rotten odor of the "sugar sickness" permeated everything throughout the home. Mercy recalled how she had tried to stifle her sobs each night by stuffing her face into the pillowcases—while the sickening smell of diabetes assaulted her nose.

Mercy remembered another neighbor in Back Valley. One day, she had angered her granny more than usual. No matter how hard she tried, Mercy could not later remember what she had done to make her granny so crazed. Giving orders to Darrell and Gary Wayne, Granny fumed, "Take 'er down the road and let 'er stay with the neighbors awhile. I can't take it no more!" Only five years old at the time, Mercy put up a full-scale battle with both her brothers. *I ain't goin' easy this time,* she thought. Kicking and screaming every step of the way, Mercy fought with all her strength. Her brothers held her tightly by each arm, dragging her feet down the dirt road, and pushed her into the neighbor's yard. She knew her brother Gary Wayne had felt sorry for her and released his grip, but Darrell held tight and pushed her forward until they reached their destination: *that* house.

Mercy hated *that* house, loathed it more than anywhere she had ever been. It was dark and dismal, even more so than her grandparents' home. Forbidden to sleep in a bed, she was forced to sleep in the baby crib. At five years of age, she had fumed and felt a terrible sense of shame and embarrassment. Again, she cried herself to sleep every night. She wet the bed, probably more than once—she could not recall.

It serves 'em right! I'm gonna pee in that bed again, jist for spite!

Her soiled sheets were hung to dry in the open yard in full view of everyone passing by, and she was humiliated. Mercy was not surprised when she was returned to Granny's. She could not understand why no one seemed to want her to live with them beyond a few days.

I reckon it's because of my sassy ways and wettin' the bed. At least, that's what Granny says.

Later, she lived with Aunt Reatha and her husband, Paul. They had two daughters, Linda and Paula, and Mercy always felt welcomed and loved.

They must like girls.

This idea was pleasing to her.

Aunt Reatha and Uncle Paul's small home on Weaver's Creek sat perched on the side of a hill, overlooking the main road to Clinchfield. Scooped from the side of the mountain, a narrow road leading to their front yard barely accommodated the width of the family's car. Mercy often feared the car ride from the main road to their house. She was certain they might stall in the creek, or slide off the mountain. The narrow front yard overlooked a steep hill and a long fall to the creek below. Mercy and her cousins were cautioned about playing too close to the drop off and the cliff that perched directly above the creek.

It was the place Daddy got mad and pushed my mommy's warshin' machine—all filled up with clothes—right over that hill. Right down into the creek. Now, what'd he do that for? He musta been drinkin' again.

Situated on the most level spot in their yard was a long, steel roller coaster, fitted with a tiny car for riding up and down the tracks. Hours were spent riding the roller coaster with her cousins, and Mercy had never felt so content with her life. Her aunt and uncle were kind, generous, loving people, and they adored one another—something she had never witnessed before. In their house, she ate popcorn straight from a dishpan on a regular basis, and was introduced to her uncle's favorite drink, Dr. Pepper. She had never tasted anything quite so good in her life. She could not remember ever having fruit with her cereal before living with them, either; each morning before school, Reatha always had bananas.

I sure am lucky to live in such a nice home. They must be rich people, cuz only rich people eat bananas.

A small, well-worn path across the creek and two log bridges led straight to her granny's house. She could visit her brothers regularly, and she relished her renewed sense of security and stability. Her aunt's home had an indoor bathroom, and Mercy delighted in the opportunity to bathe in the big bathtub on a daily basis. She recalled her aunt telling her how dirty she had been when first coming to stay with them.

I must take a bath ever day if I'm to please 'em. I want to stay here furever.

But then suddenly, she was back at her granny's house. She didn't understand why her aunt had sent her away.

Maybe cuz I didn't bathe enough, or I ate too many bananas. Or I ain't as purty as Lynn, or I was jist too sassy, or I wet the bed.

With great sorrow, Mercy returned to live with her grandparents, a sad place where she had felt neither loved nor wanted.

CHAPTER 7

GRANNY'S RULES

Granny Mattie, called Aunt Mattie by everyone who knew her, was well known throughout the surrounding areas of Clinchfield, Artrip, Cracker's Neck, and Cleveland. Standing only five feet, three inches tall, she presented a petite figure in stature only. Her tough personality, worn through the years by the trials and hardships endured on the farm, was readily apparent to those who came to know her on a personal level. On a daily basis, she twisted and wound her waist-length, raven black hair into a tight, round bun, then wrapped her whole head with a white cloth diaper, even covering her ears. This protected the family's food from germs, she would explain to anyone brave enough to question her about the diaper.

Mercy thought her granny was a little odd looking with her head wrapped up in a diaper, but she didn't dare comment about it. She didn't know which was more peculiar: the diaper on her head, or Granny's gold front tooth. To all those who knew her, Aunt Mattie was a staunch old-time Baptist, firm in her belief of "Spare the rod, spoil the child." Mercy knew her granny's rules were set in stone, with stiff penalties for those who chose to ignore them. She quickly learned the repercussions of disobeying her granny.

At the same time, her grandpaw was even harsher. Six feet tall, Daff was an intimidating figure, especially for children. With an ever-present frown on his hollow-cheeked face, he always scared Mercy.

Wearing his old, well-worn brown hat even in the presence of company, he would tilt it to the side and greet each visitor, "How's ye cats a-hoppin'?"

I reckon he don't know how to smile, does he? Maybe he forgot how to do that. And I'll never understand what that sayin' means nohow, no matter how hard I try.

From time to time, she secretly watched him eating at the dinner table, gnawing food into mush with his one tooth.

Grandpaw pulled most of his teeth with a pair o' pliers, and I don't reckon he favors wearin' his false ones. I know most mountain folks don't like doctors and don't like to take medicine. Grandpaw don't like dentists, neither.

For nearly 40 years, Uncle Daff had been a coal miner and an early member of UMWA. Once employed by Clinchfield Coal Company, he had retired from the mines, content to spend the remainder of his days on his small tobacco farm. He'd had a hard life, walking as many as 18 miles each day to and from work. In the early years, he had worked for low wages, shoveling coal from the mines. If slate was uncovered instead, he received no wages for the day. Having already raised his own seven children and a nephew, Uncle Daff had not been eager to take in R.C.'s children at this late stage in his life. His tolerance for small children had dwindled throughout the years, and he was not a man of patience. Mercy would soon learn just how little patience he had.

Mattie's and Daff's house sat on a level piece of land near the forks of the road. The intersection led to Finney, a small community to the northeast in one direction, or to Clinchfield, another tiny community to the west, and finally Cleveland to the south. Located beside the main road, it offered the family an opportunity to observe traffic moving past and a chance to wave at every car.

Their home had five rooms: two bedrooms, a living room, a kitchen, and a centrally located "sittin' room." It was rare to have an inside bathroom in Back Valley, but Mattie and Daff were fortunate to have one; thus, Granny's first rule.

(1) Don't use the bathtub! Spring water was scarce, and rainwater caught in the cinderblock cistern was not sufficient to waste on unnecessary things, they were told. Mercy would miss the daily baths in the bathtub she had grown accustomed to at Aunt Reatha's house.

(2) Don't use the inside toilet, except for emergencies! "That's for company only," Granny said, then added, "besides, that outhouse is good enough fer anybody."

(3) Don't use the toilet paper! Toilet paper was a precious commodity, a luxury most mountain folks didn't have—but Granny kept a roll just for her own use. "That's for company only!" Granny said. The outhouse was well stocked with a supply of corncobs, Sears and Roebuck catalogues, magazines, and old newspapers for the children's use.

A slop jar was stored under Granny's bed at night, in case

the weather conditions prevented anyone from making it to the outhouse. That was a rare occasion, Mercy remembered, because she always reminded herself to make a trip to the outhouse before going to bed. She was determined she wouldn't have to use that slop jar.

Not never, not never!

But she did, of course.

The family kitchen held a large, wood-burning stove, an old white enameled kitchen sink, a refrigerator, a small metal cabinet for storing dishes, and an old cupboard for making biscuits. In the middle of the room, a vinyl-covered table provided a place for eating, "lookin' beans," skimming milk, and conversing with company. Hanging over the table was a solitary, exposed light-bulb and the ever-popular flytrap. Swinging over the "eats," the trap served as a useful device for removing pesky flies and insects from Granny's spic-and-span kitchen.

It's disgustin' with all them flies: some dead, others still buzz-in' 'round and 'round, all tangled up in that sticky goo!

Grooved-planks, painted blue, surrounded the outdated kitch-en. Plastic flowered curtains draped across two windows pro-vided an air of décor and privacy. Beside the cook stove sat a small, wooden box for storing kindling and larger pieces of wood used to fire up the stove each morning before breakfast. An old, well-worn linoleum rug adorned the kitchen floor, and Granny was careful to clean and mop it on a regular basis, sometimes every day. Granny was proud of her kitchen; she was an immacu-late housekeeper and took great pride in maintaining cleanliness, specifically when she cooked. Very early on, she laid down the rules for her kitchen.

(4) Wash your hands right away when you come in the back door of the kitchen! Playing outside led to all manner of germs on their hands, Granny was sure. This rule dovetailed with the next.

(5) Don't *ever* pet animals! Granny was particularly strict about not letting any animal brush up against her, and petting animals was strictly forbidden.

(6) Never open the refrigerator door! Mercy soon learned the reason behind that rule. *There was simply nothin' in there anybody'd want. Jist fresh cow milk, buttermilk, thick cream, lots o' homemade butter, clabbered milk for makin' biscuits…and more milk, sometimes blinky with cream still floatin' on top. I ain't never seen so much milk!*

(7) Don't play with the bolt-latch! An oversized, solid wood door framed the entranceway to the kitchen. Its lock, a heavy, Daniel Boone homemade wooden latch, offered security for the family and was often an enticement for visiting children—*that is, for the ones who didn't know Granny's rules.*

(8) No snacks after supper! Mercy supposed she was like most other kids her age. She enjoyed candy bars, sugary delicacies, and pop. Having grown accustomed to them in Aunt Reatha's home, she longed for any special sweet treats. Cooking staples consisted of simple, basic ingredients for meals with few store-bought "extrys," as Granny called them. On rare occasions, the children were allowed to eat leftovers of milk and corn bread with a slice of onion, homemade biscuits with streaked meat, or cold biscuits topped with grease.

This may have been Granny's most hateful rule because a bottle o' pop was as rare as gold itself in Granny's house!

(9) Don't lean against or sit on the beds…*Never!* Mercy liked it when they all gathered in the sittin' room. The old wood and coal burning fireplace, its large mantle cluttered with a collection of knickknacks, served as the focal point, especially during harsh winters when everyone stood on the hearth to warm their "hind-ends." She'd witnessed many visitors warming their smoking rears by the fire. Two antique rockers and a couple of old cane-laced, straight-backed chairs were used when entertaining visitors. Two regular-sized beds and a twin bed filled up the rest of the room. Once the feather beds were made up in the early morning hours, no one was allowed to lean against or sit on them. Her granny was very strict about that rule!

(10) Go to bed early! The whole family slept in that room: Mercy and Granny in one bed, Darrell and Gary Wayne in another, and Grandpaw in the twin bed. Although it was a crowded room, it fit the needs of the family. An oversized velvet rug bought from a traveling peddler that depicted a family of deer was proudly displayed on one wall. Two windows, one beside Grandpaw's twin bed and another over Granny's bed, provided the only sources of light for the sittin' room. Mercy loved her sleeping spot in the room, since it was located directly beneath one of the windows. She spent many evenings watching the sun go down.

Everbody goes to bed with the chickens at this house. It's way too early for me!

There wasn't much privacy in the sittin' room for anyone. She didn't know why they all slept in the same room, but she thought it was probably to keep the rest of the house clean and to keep from having to heat the whole house during the long, cold winter months. When relatives came to visit and it was bedtime, Mercy simply put on pajamas (in another room, of course), climbed underneath the covers, said, "Good night; don't let the bed bugs bite," and eavesdropped on the others still awake while pretending to sleep. She had learned all kinds of things that way from the grownups who thought she was asleep.

(11) Don't use the living room; it's for company only! Directly inside the front door was the living room, but Mercy didn't know why they called it that—no one ever *lived* in that room. It was a strange room that held a "devanet," as her granny called the couch, an old wooden dresser and mirror, an oval coffee table, and mismatched chairs. Mercy couldn't remember the living room being used since her teachers, Mrs. Owens and Miss Smith, had made a home visit. But she would sometimes sneak in there when Granny was outside busy with chores. Simply because the room was such a mystery, she was curious to see what might be of value in there. Although there were two windows and glass in the front door, the dark, gloomy room gave Mercy a chill whenever she was brave enough to sit alone in the living room.

What's in here worth hidin'? I need to do some more plunderin' in these things to find out. Maybe it's this green glass dish, or this chicken knickknack...or maybe these old Victrola records? Is this what Granny's tryin' to hide? It can't be that picture of Jesus or John F. Kennedy. I reckon I'll never figger it out.

(12) Never, *ever* play the Victrola phonograph! Another of Granny's strictest rules had been made about her favorite antique record player. The old records simply gathered dust inside Granny's cherished piece of furniture.

Without a doubt, Mercy thought the most peculiar part of the home was the family dressing room. Not the room itself, but its contents. Granny, Grandpaw, Darrell, Gary Wayne, and Mercy all used the room for dressing and undressing.

That's about it, not much of anythin' else.

Each family member's clothing was strewn about the walls using coat hangers on nails. Mercy's designated spot was behind the door; she liked her space because it kept her clothes out of sight of visitors. The room was a modest one, with two regular beds, a trunk for storing quilts, a small shelf for organizing schoolbooks, and the mysterious *closet*.

(13) *Never* try to get into the closet! Even Grandpaw knew that rule— he was by no means permitted in there either. Just like Fort Knox, everyone said, the closet was completely impenetrable. Typical of older homes, there were no closets in any other rooms—just this one. Mercy determined that it must be a *special* closet, for an extraordinary purpose, because Granny never, ever allowed anyone to see what was inside. Never, ever. That was Granny's biggest, most serious rule. In spite of all attempts to catch a glimpse of its contents, it was impossible. Everyone knew the closet would be locked until the end of the world, and Granny carried the skeleton key. Throughout the years, every family member watched Granny taking her cherished items to the closet for safekeeping. Things like cartons of pop, bags of candy, mail, and gifts—just about everything. From time to time, Granny took a nap during the day, but she always wore her apron with the skeleton key tucked deep inside her pocket.

One day, Mercy and her brothers schemed to steal the key from Granny, but to no avail. They had tried, but their granny, a light sleeper just like the giant in "Jack and the Beanstalk," woke up in the middle of their antics.

"Y'all git outa here now. I'm tryin' to nap!"

And we all ran to the hills—certain Granny would skin our hides. I got a new purpose in life: someday I'm gonna find out whut's in that closet!

(14) Never go in the good room! This was perhaps one of Granny's strangest rules. Granny had named the bedroom beside the living room the "good room." That room was used only for overnight guests, usually couples staying for short visits. For the most part, this room remained locked. But Mercy occasionally had an opportunity to scamper into the room behind Granny. To

Mercy, it was such a puzzle: something curious about the off-limits rule that made her want to see everything in the room. Nothing appeared to be of great value to her. Only a bed, a dresser, an old cedar chifforobe, and a variety of tables were in there. A gold, Asian-style bedspread with thick tassels hung loosely on the bed. Mercy questioned her granny about the odd-looking bed cover, and learned it had been purchased from a passing peddler. Her granny's treasured Sunday-go-to-church suits and shoes were always neatly organized inside the wardrobe.

It stinks in there, anyhow. Jist the smell of mothballs and cedar.

During one of her rare visits to the good room, Mercy spied a collection of old photographs haphazardly placed on the dresser.

"Who is that woman in this here picture?" Mercy asked.

"Leave me alone now; I'm tryin' to find somethin' in this chifforobe," Granny said.

Mercy persisted. "Well, who is it?"

Turning her head around to glance sideways at Mercy, Granny said, "Which picture are ye talkin' 'bout?" When she saw the photo, Granny said, "Aw, hit's your mother, Nell."

In awe, Mercy gingerly lifted the photograph and stared longingly at it. Unable to let go of it, she held it firmly and gazed into the eyes of her birth mother. It was a brief moment; her granny soon snatched the photograph away, eager to leave the room.

As the picture slipped from her hands, Mercy protested. "But I wanna look at it!"

"Aw, you don't need to look at it. Now git outa here!" Granny snapped.

From that moment on, Mercy would beg to have any opportunity to enter the good room for a chance to gaze at her mother's old photograph. With the passing of time, she often found herself unable to call up a clear image of her mother's face.

Throughout the years, she would have rare glimpses of the small, distorted picture, but she treasured the feeling of knowing something belonging to her mother was secretly tucked away in the good room.

"Climbing"
Ella Wheeler Wilcox

Who climbs the mountain does not always climb.
The winding road slants downward many a time;
Yet each descent is higher than the last.
Has thy path fallen? That will soon be past.
Beyond the curve the way leads up and on.
Think not thy goal forever lost or gone.
Keep moving forward; if thine aim is right
Thou canst not miss the shining mountain height.
Who would attain to summits still and fair,
Must nerve himself through valleys of despair.

CHAPTER 8

ON THE ROAD AGAIN

By now, Mercy was promoted to the second grade at Cleveland Elementary. Her teacher, Miss Bessie, was a typical old schoolmarm who had never married. And Mercy was certain she knew *why*: she was just too darn mean! Mean as a striped snake! Miss Bessie carried a large poke filled with a change of clothing on a daily basis.

Now why does she do that? She's a quare old woman...maybe even more quare than Granny.

By no means did Miss Bessie ever smile. With the exception of the faded, red and brown, wool scarf she wore, Miss Bessie had no room for frills or color. Her cotton hose and black, laced-up shoes with wedge heels and high tops exemplified her no-nonsense personality. With a tall, gangly, rough frame, she was intimidating, a stern disciplinarian in the classroom. From time to time, Miss Bessie would pop pupils on the head or ears when they missed an answer to her question.

Mercy's time came sooner than she expected. *See Spot Run* was a dull book, and she tired quickly of the boring words. *See Spot run. See Spot jump. See Spot. Spot. Here, Spot.* She hated it. Startled, Mercy jumped as Miss Bessie's pencil popped her ear, and she heard Miss Bessie's threatening voice, "I knew you wouldn't be any good from the first time you walked through this school-room door!"

Insecure and not brave enough to respond, Mercy took this abuse—but she would long recall those hurtful, biting words.

I'll show Ole Miss Bessie. You jist wait an' see. Maybe I'll jist steal her old watch, the one with the huge face as big as a silver dollar, the one with the lil' band. It ain't a bit purty nohow! I hate See Spot Run—*and I ain't got no use for ole Miss Bessie! One day she'll git her comeuppance.*

Relief from Miss Bessie's class came unexpectedly. Mercy moved to Ohio with her daddy in the middle of the school year, and she could not have been more thrilled. She wondered if her granny and grandpaw had asked him to come and take her away because she was just too much trouble, ate too much, or was too sassy. She never quite knew the real reason her daddy came for her, nor did she care. Mercy idolized him and was happy to be by his side. She had not seen him on a regular basis while living with her granny and grandpaw.

She couldn't know what her father's plans would be for her.

For a brief period, she lived with a young couple named George and Pat. Although they were kind people, Mercy was leery and suspicious of both of them. George and Pat lived in the city limits of Manchester, a tiny, unpretentious town on the banks of the Ohio

River, just across the border of Kentucky. Mercy had never experienced sidewalks before; they were far different from the gravel and dirt roads she had grown so familiar with back in the mountains. She often skipped across the sidewalk cracks chanting, "Step on a crack, break your mother's back." Mercy was unsure if that was what she really wanted to happen to her mother, so she never, ever stepped on the cracks—unless she was angry, recalling the day her mother had abandoned her. During those times, she stepped forward carefully, deliberately stomping on each crack in the sidewalk. She always wondered if her mother's back, wherever she might be, was now broken, perhaps even into tiny pieces.

The couple's small three-room house sat directly in front of the sidewalk. With no front yard, Mercy ran and played in their large, fenced-in backyard. She missed the opportunities to play house in the woods; she longed for the freedom of her beloved mountains. But she knew they were far from her reach, and she soon adjusted to the new school, new friends, and strange sounds of the small town.

One day, all dressed in her Sunday-go-to-church clothes, Mercy was escorted into a stranger's office by George and Pat. Unaware of why she had come to visit the well-dressed gentleman, she respectfully listened to his litany of questions. At some point during the conversation, Mercy realized the depth of what was occurring. This well-groomed stranger, called an attorney, wanted to know, "Would you like to be adopted?"

This was the first time she had heard the word *adopted*, and she was horrified at the thought of separation from her father. As the realization of what was about to occur sank in, she screamed, "No! No! No!" and ran sobbing from the room.

Later, Mercy packed her clothes and left George and Pat's home.

Maybe because I didn't wanna leave my daddy or maybe I was jist bein' sassy, like Granny always says. Or maybe I wasn't as purty as my sister, Lynn. I don't know, and I don't care! I love my daddy, and I aim not to leave 'im! Daddy takes me everywhere with 'im, and he loves me. I know he does. Ain't nobody else ever loved me, not ever, jist my daddy. But why'd he wanna give me away to them people? He does love me, don't he?

Once again, she moved to another home in Manchester. Living in her cousin Gay's home, she learned lots of new practical skills during that year. It was there that she first began to enjoy reading. She would read, reread, and then reread again her favorite fairytale, "Rumpelstiltskin." Mercy was completely astonished by the love of the mother, who was willing to do whatever was necessary for her child to be returned. Mercy knew she would never be so fortunate.

Why'd she love her lil' baby so much? I jist don't understand. My mommy sure don't love me like that.

For the first time in her short life, Mercy questioned the authenticity of God. Determined to get an answer, she questioned her daddy. "How do you know there's a real God if you can't see him? How do you know he's up there in heaven? Why can't we see him?" Mercy recognized he was uncomfortable with the depth of the questions, but her daddy, in his own way, had responded as best he could. She thought it was a special time between daddy and daughter.

I reckon he ain't had much practice teachin' about God and goin' to church.

She learned to ride a bicycle and spent hours riding on the sidewalks and streets throughout the neighborhood. All on her own, she learned to swim that summer. Later, she could not recall details, but on one occasion while she was in a boat on the Ohio

River, someone simply picked her up, threw her overboard, and hollered, "Swim!"

And she did.

Even at that age, one thing Mercy had learned to do was survive. The more challenges she met, the more strong-willed and determined she became to overcome any obstacle placed in her path.

At some point in time, Mercy moved to Esta's house—but thankfully, she remained in the same school. Each morning at the crack of dawn, she woke up and readied herself for school. She couldn't remember anyone else being awake in the mornings as she searched for clean clothing, dressed herself, brushed her hair, and ran out the door. Each morning, as regular as clockwork, she stopped by her best friend's home and knocked on the door, where she was greeted by her friend's father. He was a kind man, she remembered. Every morning, there they were, having breakfast as a family; she thought her friend was especially lucky. They were a good Catholic family, she could tell. With genuine kindness, they provided breakfast for her each morning, not inviting her to sit at the table with them, but always bringing her toast, hot cocoa, or a small tidbit of something to eat. Mercy always wondered *why* they hadn't invited her to sit at the table with them, but she never asked, simply grateful for their generosity.

Within walking distance from Esta's house was her father's favorite bar. Hopping and skipping down the now-familiar sidewalks, Mercy often made the trip to the tavern. Sitting on a barstool beside her daddy, she sipped bottles of Nehi Orange and chewed on her favorite Mounds candy bar. Mercy loved watching her daddy laugh and drink along with the other town boozers. When she whined or begged to go home, her daddy gave her a handful of quarters to play country music on the jukebox—and she learned to dance the Pony, the latest craze. Right there in front of all the men at the bar, she danced away, jumping and twirling, as her audience clapped boisterously for each performance. Mercy had never been happier.

By the end of her third-grade year, she found herself with a new half-brother. The baby was named Gary Wayne; she just couldn't understand why she now had two brothers with the same name. Mercy thought he was an adorable baby, with his curly brown locks and bright hazel eyes.

I guess Daddy jist fergot to tell Esta he already had one boy named Gary Wayne. The name don't make no difference to me, though.

When the baby was three months old, her daddy made the decision to send her back to her mountains to live with Granny and Grandpaw again in Back Valley. Mercy was confused; it was beyond her youthful understanding. She knew her daddy was a truck driver and was unable to take her on the road with him. But she wanted to live with him every single day.

By this time, Mercy had moved in and out of way too many homes of strangers and relatives since her mother had left her. Mercy finally learned why she had not been permitted the luxury of living with her Aunt Reatha and Uncle Paul on a permanent basis: Aunt Reatha had been pregnant, and they now had a new baby boy named Ronnie. Suspecting she had not been wanted because she was a girl, she accepted her mind's rationale. She had already acknowledged the insignificance of being born female, since it was entrenched in everyday life and everything around her seemed to support the idea.

I reckon boys are just loved more, and I reckon I must be a really bad child. Or jist too ugly and sassy.

Her lack of trust and fears of being abandoned were now firmly part of who Mercy had become. Although she cherished the mountains, she dreaded returning to follow Granny's rules.

CHAPTER 9

GRANNY'S FAVORITE

From that point forward, Mercy heard these words from Granny on a regular basis: "If you don't *mind*, we're gonna send you to that orphanage in Grundy!" Hearing those words stung her heart, and dread dogged her steps; she didn't *want* to move, not ever again. Longing for stability and a sense of security, she begged and pleaded with her daddy not to be sent to "the home." As she now saw him only once a year, she was unable to communicate with him very often. She knew he couldn't shelter her from the harsh treatment she endured on Granny and Grandpaw's farm.

Why don't Granny and Grandpaw love me like they love my brothers, Darrell and Gary Wayne? I try my best to act like a good girl. I reckon I'm jist too much trouble, bein' a girl and all, and not bein' old enough to fend for myself. I'll do jist that some-day. Someday.

As Granny and Grandpaw reminded her of how much trouble she was, how much food she ate, and how they were giving her a good home, she felt unworthy, undeserving of anyone's love. On an everyday basis, Mercy witnessed the affection her granny lavished on her brother, Darrell, when he was given special treats. He gloated about the adoration and special attention he received, fully recognizing Granny made a difference between the kids.

Store-bought, canned goods were a rarity at their table; home-grown vegetables were canned from the farm and stored in a pantry in the sittin' room, or in the cellar underneath the milk house.

Darrell loved canned, store-bought food, especially spaghetti, and Granny would periodically purchase a can. Of course, it was just for Mercy's older brother, Darrell—the spoiled one, the pampered one, the mean brother she had grown to loathe because of her jealousy.

Mercy instinctively knew when special food was placed on the dinner table that neither she nor Gary Wayne would be allowed to eat it. Not even a single bite.

"But Granny, why can't I have some to eat?" she pleaded.

Gary Wayne would join in, "Well, I want some too. I love spaghetti!"

"Y'all can't have none because I said so. That's Darrell's food!" Granny snapped.

No matter how often they begged, Granny would emphasize it was Darrell's food. Mercy and Gary Wayne would sullenly watch, simply staring as Darrell devoured the food, not offering to share, a smug smile painted on his face.

On birthdays, Granny baked a special cake for him, but seldom for her and Gary Wayne. They had learned to sit silently and watch him eat; they had grown accustomed to the preferential treatment, feeling helpless to alter Granny's ways. Gary Wayne received special attention from Grandpaw; so, Mercy came to realize there was no one who loved her in that special way—except maybe her daddy, and he was living in Michigan. She reminded herself again to be a good girl, to do well in school, not to complain about the chores, and to make her grandparents proud of her accomplishments. Maybe then she could win their affection.

Settling back into life on the tobacco farm, Mercy begged her granny to let her make a new playhouse, not in the woods this time. She had tired of playing house in the woods alone. Her granny found one for her: the chicken house. Mercy found great pleasure in her make-believe world, and set out to make the chicken house as home-like as she could. With great pride and a sense of purpose, she shoveled piles of chicken manure to ready the wooden floors for her own special place. It took hours of hard work, shoveling and hauling the chicken droppings from inside the tiny building to sprinkle on the family garden. And Mercy was proud to contribute something to the family's chores.

"It makes fer good fertilizer," said Granny.

Finally, Mercy placed wooden stools and mismatched castaway benches inside for comfort. With the art of a seasoned interior decorator, she hung worn-out plastic curtains on the single window, an addition that contributed to the ambience of a real house. Satisfied with her new home, she spent hours playing with her doll, conversing with her world of imaginary friends and sipping from a miniature teacup. Often lonesome for company, she pleaded with Gary Wayne to play with her, as she knew Darrell would refuse. At times, it was necessary to bargain with her brother.

In a childlike, pleading voice, Mercy begged, "Gary Wayne, will you play house with me? Please. Please." She sensed he would not likely turn her away.

"Well, I reckon I could," Gary Wayne said, and as his bashful smile crept across his face, he added, "but only if'n you play Cowboys-n-Indians with me later."

The same old bargain between brother and sister had always worked for them. Mercy and Gary Wayne enjoyed spending time together as brother and sister; they enjoyed one another's company inside the chicken house, and shooting miniature pistols in their make-believe world of fun and imagination. Although the chicken house was fun, the *real* world awaited Mercy in the fourth grade.

CHAPTER 10

CLEVELAND ELEMENTARY

It was in fourth grade where Mercy met her first challenge in school: multiplication tables. Frustrated at her own ineptitude, she detested learning the new skill. Most of her friends had already memorized the mysterious, cryptic tables. On a regular basis, Mrs. Cupp, the teacher for that year, held up large multiplication flash cards in front of the class and randomly called on pupils for answers. Everyone dreaded this activity, especially Mercy.

One day I'm gonna be the laughin' stock of this whole classroom! I jist know it. I jist know it! Everybody else knows the 0s, they all know the 1s, but there's jist too many silly numbers to memorize. How will I ever learn this stuff? I reckon I'm jist a peckerhead.

One day finally came. Mrs. Cupp prowled the classroom aisles, peered down overtop her black-framed glasses and slowly smiled. "Mercy, what is 9 times 7?"

Clasping her hands nervously across her lap, Mercy slid her fingers under the desk, flicked her fingertips back and forth, and tried to solve the problem. It was no use. "Um, I reckon I don't hardly know that one," she said, and she lowered her face downward into herself.

Raising her head up and straightening her back for a more rigid stance, and pushing her breath through clenched teeth, Mrs. Cupp hissed, "You know you should know all these by now. We've been working on these tables for three weeks. Have you studied any of them at all?"

"Mrs. Cupp, I did study. Well, I studied a right smart." Slowly Mercy hung her head, as warmth caressed her cheeks.

"Well, since you don't know the answer, I'll just go on to someone else."

As Mrs. Cupp walked away, Mercy vowed to herself that she would memorize those wicked multiplication tables for the next time her teacher challenged her. She went home and studied over and over, and over again, until she was finally confident in herself.

By the end of the weekend, Mercy had learned all of them; she felt the accomplishment of this huge feat was a turning point in her life. With an inner drive and the need to make her grandparents proud, she recognized that with hard work and perseverance, she could succeed in school.

Not only did Mercy strive to do well in all her classes, she also wanted to be a well-behaved child, especially in school. She was frightened of the in-school suspension room used for unruly students at Cleveland Elementary. It was located outside the school, not on the inside. A tiny space with chicken wire sides, the caged-in space held a straight-backed wooden chair, and the door was held shut with a lock on the outside. Each morning and afternoon, buses passed by the little space, and every student, teacher, and parent in the community had a view of the naughty student assigned to that little chicken coop on any given day.

I never, ever wanna go to that place, but I reckon my cousin Burrhopper set up housekeepin' there. It seems like he's always in trouble, always standin' or wilin' away the hours outside, sittin' on the straight-backed chair in that little cage.

Mercy felt bad for her cousin, and she wondered if he was allowed to eat lunch in that little birdcage. She knew most kids carried bagged lunches to school. But Mercy noticed the well-to-do kids went to the high school for lunch: a short bus ride around the bends of the river road, across the bridge, through downtown, and up the hill to the high school that overlooked the small town of Cleveland.

Mercy wanted to show everyone she wasn't poor. Methodically planning her first big trip to the high school cafeteria, she hoarded her money and set the date for the event; it would be a Friday, of course, which was hot dog day. She wouldn't ask for her granny's permission, since she knew it wouldn't be granted. The day arrived, and Mercy patiently waited in line with the other kids who could afford to eat daily in the cafeteria. She was so proud. Yet at the same time, she was petrified in this new environment. Rowdy high school students swarmed the large, open cafeteria. Scampering for their lunch trays, they shoveled down their food and chatted loudly with friends across the tables. Mercy had never experienced such chaos, but she relished the new experience and felt a sense of renewed freedom. All by herself, she had planned, saved her money and was now eating a hot dog with high school students. With tremendous satisfaction, she paid her 25 cents and devoured her chili-onions-mustard hot dog. Mercy was confident she had crossed another threshold in her short lifetime.

Mercy felt even more experienced and independent when the next school year began in fifth grade. This was to be her last year at the elementary school, and she was proud to be one of the older students in the school. But these learning experiences would be very different.

How small them lil' first graders look over there. I sure do feel sorry for them. They got a lotta learnin' to do. All that readin'. And Lordy, them multiplication tables!

But this year, Mercy's classroom was different. It was divided into two grade levels: two rows for the fourth grade, and two rows for the fifth grade. She won her first spelling bee that year, with the word *restaurant*, and she was proud of her achievement. But she wasn't proud of the song she had to sing in the 4-H competition that year: "Wolverton Mountain." It was the only song she knew, and she had sung it up and down the roads in Back Valley. Standing in front of the crowd of adults, she had belted out the song, hoping no one would realize she'd missed a word or two.

Maybe them adults don't know that song. But all in all, I did good, I reckon. I wouldn't a done it if they hadn't pushed me out on that stage, though. I did forget some of the words. Can't carry a tune in a bucket.

Occasionally they would have birthday parties in the classroom, with parents bringing cupcakes or a cake to all the students in a class. Those were the well-to-do kids, Mercy knew, so she never expected the surprise party her friends gave her. For her birthday, they brought extra snacks from home and gave them to her during lunch. Since she'd never had a birthday party, she was more than pleased with the candy and sweets given to her on her special day.

There's always a surprise at this school. Ever day is a treat for me.

Sometimes students surprised their teachers. This year, Mercy's class shocked Miss Easterly with a Roll Up Party. Vowing to keep their secret, students planned and plotted their surprise, and at the chosen time, all the students yelled, "Surprise!" and leaned under their desks, grabbed their hidden fruit, and swiftly rolled the apples and oranges down the aisle, toward the front of the classroom.

It was a strange lil' party. Well, except when Ranzy tried to roll his banana down the aisle. Don't he know bananas can't roll? What was he thinkin'? Boys are always doin' strange things.

Then she remembered her latest attempt at a new hairdo. Mercy's hair had grown past her shoulders; she had been proud of her long, brown hair. Each morning she tediously brushed away the overnight tangles, pulled her hair into a ponytail atop her head, and then coiffed it into a tight, round bun held in place with tiny pins. She was convinced her new hairstyle made her look sophisticated—until the day Moonpie said it looked like a cow pile! Mercy had been devastated. Humiliated, she had tattled to the teacher and reminded herself to be more careful about wearing the cow pile to school.

The incident had not swayed her love for school, though, since she'd rather be there than anywhere else. She enjoyed the everyday academic challenges and making new friends. At the end of each school day, dread cast its dark shadow around her. She knew her grandpaw was well aware of how much she loved school, and he often threatened to punish her by not allowing her to go to school the next day if she was too sassy. To Mercy, this was the absolute worst punishment she could ever receive.

Each day after school, Mercy's granny kept her overloaded with chores, insisting she stay busy, especially if she found Mercy sitting. Granny would grab a broom, stick it in her hand and say, "Find somethin' to do; ain't no lollygaggin' 'round here!"

Mercy found life on the farm to be endless drudgery. There was always more work to do: dishes to wash, hogs to slop, kindling to chop, wood and coal to carry, or another row to hoe in the garden.

CHAPTER 11

HOG-KILLIN'

One of Mercy's goals was to receive the perfect attendance award for this school year, but hog killing day was a special day in the mountains. *Everyone* missed school. Being absent on this day was common, since most farm kids worked alongside their families in the enormous task of working up the meat. Four or five hogs were sometimes slaughtered in a single day, and neighbors gathered to help one another. It was an exciting social event for everyone involved.

Since frigid temperatures were necessary to keep the meat from spoiling during its preparation, Mercy's granny carefully pored over the almanac to select one of the coldest days in November. On this chosen day, Mercy rose before daylight to the cheerful sound of neighbors in the front lot. Jumping from her feather tick bed, she carefully selected work clothes for the day ahead and scampered to the front door, peeking outside at the activities which had already started without her. Neighbors were moving in different directions throughout the lot: building fires under the iron kettle of water, bracing the teepee of poles to be used for hanging the carcass, whetting long-bladed knives, and gathering wood or other tools and utensils.

A short time later, she knew it was time for the slaughtering. For Mercy, that was the worst time of the whole day. She grew sad at the thought of what must be done to enjoy bacon, ham, and tenderloin throughout the year. She closed her eyes and placed her hands tightly over her ears, trying to drown out the high-pitched squeals as the hogs were shot. Once their throats were cut to drain the blood, each hog was dipped into scalding water inside a huge barrel. It was then hoisted by a pulley fastened to the rear legs so that it hung head-down beneath the pole teepee. Hairs were scraped meticulously from the steaming carcass. Mercy watched wide-eyed as each pig was slit down the middle and the offal removed; she kept herself preoccupied with mundane thoughts to avoid thinking about the food chain and why all this was necessary.

Backbones, ribs, pork chops, head, feet, and ears were removed and laid out on a makeshift table. Mercy helped trim fat from the shoulders for her granny to make sausage for freezing and canning. She loved souse, although she sometimes shuddered when she was reminded of its origins: the head, feet, and ears. Later, cracklings were rendered from lard to be used in corn bread and fried potatoes.

For hours, roaring fires were kept ablaze. For a mid-day meal, Mercy and her brothers sneaked hefty chunks of fresh tenderloin and skewered them on sticks, roasting them over the fire and gobbling down the juicy morsels. Mercy had eaten entirely too much and her stomach rolled, queasy from the odors of freshly cooked meat and the rancid smells from the early slaughtering process. She knew the same smells would linger for days inside the house, permeate the cracks in the walls, and settle into their clothing. It happened every year.

Mercy turned to watch her grandpaw devour his favorite midday meal of fried brains. Mixed with eggs and fried in a skillet, hog brains were considered a delicacy. Nausea welled inside her again as she watched him eat something she considered to be a sacred, untouchable part of the freshly killed hog. She thought her grandpaw eccentric, perhaps even deviant, as she continued to watch him finish the portion—and sop his plate.

I'll never, ever, ever eat anythin' like that. What kinda quare man would eat brains anyhow!

Throughout the long day, Mercy and her brothers had passed the time throwing a hog bladder to one another across the creek. It was a ritual they enjoyed each year. Blown up with a hollowed-out reed, it was inflated like a balloon and tied shut. They didn't own a ball, so it made for an interesting game of catch-the-bladder-before-it-busts.

That night, Mercy fell asleep dreaming about the slaughtered hog with its severed head, body hanging from the gallows and fried brains dancing in her mind. Squealing from excruciating pain, each pig grunted guttural sounds solely understood by others of its own kind. At the same time, each head turned toward her, gorged eyes staring at her, beseeching her to rescue it from its untimely torture.

Wakened from her sleep early the next morning, Mercy consoled herself that it had been an exciting event worth the nightmares she had just experienced. She was eager to return to school and share all the things she had witnessed during hog-killing day on the farm.

Excerpt From "The Common People"
Ella Wheeler Wilcox

I like the common people,
Who have not wealth, or fame,
Who own no greater riches
Than a humble home and name,
Among these unknown toilers
In life's great thronged marts—
I find the deepest thinkers—
I find the truest hearts.

CHAPTER 12

OVERNIGHT STAYS

Mercy was happy-go-lucky when she socialized with her three friends: Barbara Ann, Linda Joann, and Gail. She viewed all of them as rich kids. Barbara Ann lived in a two-story brick home on Mill Creek, Gail's parents owned a new brick home near Reeds Valley, and her cousin Linda Joann lived in downtown Cleveland, close to all the stimulation only city life could offer.

Imagine that, a brick house! Not like my house, covered with tar paper that was supposed to look like brick, but a real brick house.

Mercy knew her home could not compare to the luxuries found in her friends' homes: things like electric stoves, indoor bathrooms everyone was allowed to use, separate bedrooms, all the niceties she coveted. She remembered that friends were not allowed to spend the night at her house. Mercy recalled in earlier years a cousin who had come to spend the night with her; Grandpaw sent the girl home. Humiliated and embarrassed, she had not repeated that mistake.

When Mercy had questioned her grandpaw, he simply said, "I've got 'nuff mouths to feed. I don't need another'n!"

She had never broached the subject again. By this time, she had become thick-skinned, and knew her grandpaw's hard-nosed rule was set in stone.

Later, after pleading over and over again, Mercy was given permission to enjoy a once-a-year-sleepover at a selected friend's house. She loved the idea of spending just one night in a home of luxury. Struggling with the decision of where to stay for that single night each year was tough; she was not adept at making decisions for herself.

Should I stay in downtown Cleveland this year to go trick-or-treatin' with Linda Joann, or with Barbara Ann for her yearly pajama party?

A smile broke across Mercy's face. She remembered last year's Halloween night away from home had been spent at her Aunt Mildred's house in downtown Cleveland. She had walked side-by-side with her cousins, Linda, Judy, and Carl, and they had soaped all the store windows in town. Anyone who had not responded to their knock at the door got a good dose of soapy windows. They had ventured into all the local stores and downtown neighborhoods for all the candy they could wish for. Afterward, they had eaten their fill of miniature chocolates and butterscotch candies late into the night.

CHAPTER 13

NOVEMBER 22

In 1963, Mercy began a new adventure in sixth grade at the newly constructed Cleveland High School. Located on the outskirts of Cleveland, the imposing structure was a harsh contrast to the hills surrounding it. The two-story brick building, with its new gymnasium, auditorium, and state-of-the-art classrooms, brought a sense of connection and pride to the community. Mercy felt privileged to be among the first students to attend the new school.

On November 22, shocking news squawked over the intercom: "John F. Kennedy has been shot!" Students stopped working and stared open-mouthed at the teacher, Mrs. Bailey. Silence engulfed the classroom as Mercy's teacher stared at the intercom. Even at such a young age, the students realized the seriousness of the situation, and glanced about the room, quizzical expressions on their faces. The radio continued its minute-by-minute commentaries, teaching halted, and friends began to whisper throughout the room. Finally, they heard the ominous words: "President John F. Kennedy is dead." Overwhelmed with it all, Mercy cried. Instinctively she realized this was an event she would remember for years to come.

November 22 was also Barbara Ann's birthday, and Mercy was spending her one night away from home on Mill Creek that night. Early that morning, she had readied her finest shoes and bloomers for the overnight stay. She had reminded herself to pack her nicest clothes so no one would figure out how poor she was.

Aunt Reatha always said, "You make sure you have on your best underwear, you never know when you might be in a car accident!"

Mercy had never forgotten that advice, so she made sure she packed her best just in case of that accident. She knew she would have to get undressed at some point during the night, and she wanted everyone at the pajama party to see her new pajamas, purchased just for this occasion.

Mercy guessed Granny and Grandpaw knew her friends' parents were well-to-do; that's why they made such a big deal out of her wearing her best. All the fuss about taking her nicest things only reinforced to her that she was probably one of those "poor kids off the mountain," just like everyone said.

"It's a different kind of party this year cuz I'm invitin' boys!" Barbara Ann quipped.

What a great idea. Boys at a party! I've never been to a party with boys and girls. Besides, I've never had a birthday party, so I don't have no idea what to expect.

During the party, Mercy felt mature and worldly, with only a hint of seeming out of place. Throughout the afternoon, she and her friends played tag and softball in the field behind Barbara Ann's house. After overindulging on popcorn and chocolate fudge, the small group settled into Barbara Ann's living room. It was time to play spin the bottle. Mercy thought that was a strange name for a game, but she listened carefully to all the rules. The object of the game appeared to be to kiss someone of the opposite sex.

Oh, Lord A- mercy! I've never kissed a boy before. Lord have mercy on me!!

She felt flushed and anxious thinking about what was coming: her first kiss. Not remembering all the details of the night because of all the excitement, she later recalled how the bottle had stopped directly in front of her. Not wanting to appear unsophisticated, she had soared from her chair and scampered into the nearby-darkened room to receive her first grown-up kiss from her friend Terry.

And I sure got it, right on the mouth, that afternoon at Barbara Ann's birthday party! It'll be a memory forever held in my mind. I ain't sure it was a good experience, but I'll never forget it.

Back home the next day, Mercy decided it was time to relinquish her chicken house. She had received her first kiss, and felt she was on her way to becoming a woman. She was too mature now for her playhouse in the old chicken coop. Propagation of the chickens had triggered the house to be overrun with new doodies. It was time to let them come home again. But she would annoy them at every opportunity. It was her job to put the chickens up for the night. Each evening after checking for new eggs in the nests, but before she closed their door for the night, she sang to them. She accidentally learned they didn't like high-pitched music.

Oh, Lordy, they must've overheard me singin' "Wolverton

Mountain. "

With strange, erratic movements, all the chickens cocked their heads and clucked with obvious distaste and agitation at hearing her song. The first time she had performed the sonata, they squawked, flew out of the yard, and did a chicken dance around the side of the hill. Knowing that, she sang a screeching lullaby to them every night and laughed and giggled at their reaction.

CHAPTER 14

BAPTIZIN' AT CARBO

Periodically, Mercy attended services at Weaver's Creek Baptist Church near her home. No other family members went with her to church, but she enjoyed the solitude of the short walk and sometimes chatting with relatives and neighbors along the route. In the past, she had attended Bible School during the summers, and gained an inner peace knowing that God was always at her side. During one of the Baptist revivals, she dedicated her life to God and followed her heart to salvation: she was "saved." Following the ritual of the Baptist faith, she made plans for baptism.

Shortly thereafter, she was baptized by Preacher Kiser in the Clinch River at Carbo. She had begged her granny to attend the baptism, but to no avail. Mercy felt wounded and confused. Filled with her newfound love of God, she found it difficult to understand why her granny refused to attend the life-altering ceremony, or even to recognize the significance of this important event in her life. Realizing both her grandparents professed to be staunch Baptists confused her even further.

Mercy walked the short distance to the "head lane," the T-shaped fork in the road near their home, and hitched a ride with neighbors. Mercy attended her baptism alone. It would be a memorable day, one filled with mixed emotions, a day she would recall throughout her life.

Members of her church, as well as some visitors, stood reverently along the banks of the Clinch River, quietly observing the sanctity of the ceremony. Mercy patiently waited in line with others for her turn. Upon the preacher's command, she stepped forward with renewed faith and hope: hope that God would protect and love her as he had all mankind. Grasping her nose and covering her mouth, the preacher lifted his other hand into the air, then immersed her head in the murky river water—and she was cleansed of all her sins.

Proudly wearing her lavender raincoat over her church dress, Mercy stepped onto the banks of the Clinch river. Her cousin Sylvie welcomed her with open arms and words of encouragement.

An elderly woman, Sylvie was one of Mercy's favorite relatives. She would be forever grateful for Sylvie's thoughtful act that day. But she was again reminded that no matter how hard she attempted to be a good girl, her grandparents still were not proud of her. Neither Granny nor Grandpaw had accompanied her to one of the most important, memorable events of her life so far.

I'll never be good enough. How quare! Good enough for God, but not good enough for Granny or Grandpaw.

CHAPTER 15

PLUNDERIN'

By now, Mercy had gained an additional chore of packing three lunches each morning before going to school, one for herself and one for each of her brothers. Ashamed to continue carrying biscuits in their lunches (*because only the poor kids did that anymore*), the kids pleaded with Granny to buy them sandwich bread. Granny and Grandpaw considered "light bread" a frivolous indulgence, as they always had an endless supply of corn bread, pone bread, and biscuits.

"It costs too much!" they both argued.

In the past, Granny had proudly placed light bread on the table—but only for company, of course. When the kids grabbed slices of the special treat, they felt the force of Granny's scornful glare across the table. Darrell pleaded and pleaded with Granny, and she finally gave in to furnishing the light bread.

Gary Wayne loved brown sugar tucked between two slices of that fancy light bread. But Mercy preferred her daily lettuce, with large dollops of mayonnaise wedged between two slices of that light bread. Not biscuits, but light bread. She was pleased that other students would no longer look at her lunch and consider her so poor.

~~~

Her grandpaw seldom undertook the twelve-mile trip to Lebanon. Other neighbors had not traveled out of the valley in years, so Mercy knew that was not unusual. When necessary, her grandpaw visited the grocery store in Lebanon for free hog food. Outdated breads, cakes, and other baked products were often donated to farmers for mixing with hog feed. Mercy and her brothers always celebrated when the sack of goodies was delivered—and gobbled up everything they could, until they were stuffed. Later, their grandparents scolded them for stealing the cakes meant for the hogs.

And bein' foundered ain't a good feelin', neither. Stomach rollin', churnin', everythin' jist ready to come right up. Why, it's worse than that time I foundered on lettuce 'n onions mixed with bacon grease! But it was worth eatin' them cakes. I never thought about me eatin' up the hog slop.

Granny seldom traveled outside the valley either, but when she did, Mercy and her brothers loved plundering through the house. Since Granny was always hiding things, they were determined to find anything that might be interesting when she made her once-a-year shopping jaunt to Lebanon. After listening to Granny's strict instructions not to get into anything and promising to behave, Mercy and her brothers immediately planned their first plundering tactics.

Granny's leavin' for the day! Grandpaw plans to be gone all day, too. Aunt Reatha's visitin' and she's made plans to be gone a pretty good while. That's like music to my ears! I'll get lots of plunderin' done. We'll jist get into that brown sugar while she's gone! Granny'll be mad as a wet hen! But I love lickin' on them big lumps o' brown sugar, and I know she's got at least two boxes. I reckon I'll eat about anythin' sweet.

All three children waited until the sound of the car engine faded away down the river road, and promptly sprang into action. They went straight to the white metal cupboard just inside the kitchen door; there sat the two boxes of sugar. Grabbing one box, they hacked off 3 huge lumps, one for each of them. Mercy hoped they could convince Granny she'd really had only one box of brown sugar left in the cabinet. Throughout the day, they licked and licked their lumps of brown sugar and then licked some more.

Later, Mercy felt nauseated and had a sore tongue but still tried to finish her fist-size block of sugar. She didn't want any evidence left when Granny returned. They all knew their granny would be furious with them, so they very carefully cleaned up their mess of brown sugar droppings on the floor.

Late in the afternoon, Granny returned with Aunt Reatha in tow. Mercy had dreaded seeing them come home for hours, and she cringed at the thought of Granny's no-doubt scornful glance and searching eyes.

Can she smell that brown sugar on my breath? I don't know how, but Granny's got a keen sense of when somethin' ain't right.

Sure enough, Granny somehow knew! Mercy could tell by the way her eyes darted to and fro across the kitchen. Piercing black eyes surveyed every nook and cranny for evidence that something had been moved, even ever so slightly, anything that had been touched or was out of place. She walked straight to the white metal cupboard and immediately recognized something was missing.

"I know y'all been in that brown sugar, one whole box is a' missin'!" Granny yelled, standing in front of the open metal cabinet doors. "Whur'd it go? Whur is it?" she demanded.

All three kids lied, naturally. As if someone had declared one-two-three-go, they said in unison, "We ain't seen it! We ain't seen it! We swear."

Mercy couldn't remember her granny ever being so mad. She ranted and raved, then ranted and raved some more and called all the neighbors in Back Valley to relate the story about "all them kids gettin' into my sugar!"

All three kids ran to hide on the North Hill.

Frustrated with Granny's complaining, Aunt Reatha came to the kids' rescue. "Aw, Mother, I don't believe they got into anything. You just had one box o' sugar, remember? Besides, I picked you up another box today at Piggly Wiggly."

Lordy, thank goodness for Aunt Reatha! Granny don't get as mad when company's 'round. Why, we even went in the good room and tried gettin' into the closet. If Granny knowed that, she'd have a conniption fit for sure!

CHAPTER 16

CONNECTED TO THE WORLD

Mercy began to develop a longing to read, to devour any written material. During the school year, the library offered a wide selection of books—but during the summer months, she was lost without the comfort of the written word. Not being very selective, she supposed she had read as many *True Love Story* magazine articles as any adult. Of course, she always hid them from Granny, since she knew they would be trashed or burned. On occasion, Mercy returned to finish a story only to discover Granny had found her latest hiding place and had burned the magazines. She was determined that her enjoyment of reading would not be dampened by this unwarranted censorship.

I'll jist be more careful to hide 'em in a better spot.

"You're saved now; it's a sin to read them nasty books!" her granny always said. Maybe it is, Mercy thought. She wasn't sure, but the desire to read *something* somehow filled a void in her life. Transcending time and space, she could escape into make-believe worlds, travel to faraway places, and interact with the characters inside the stories. Uncle Lawrence and Aunt Kathleen regularly brought outdated magazines, newspapers, and journals for her to read.

I ain't sure I believe in all them alien theories in the Star *and* Enquirer*, but it sure makes for some good readin'.*

Mercy yearned for a better connection with the outside world, since she felt suffocated and stifled by the restrictions of the mountain world around her. She and her brothers longed for a television at home. Darrell and Gary Wayne tired of the one-night-a-week trip to watch Hitchcock movies at Aunt Reatha's house. Mercy was not given permission to go, of course, because she was a girl. Eventually, her daddy surprised them by sending money to Granny and Grandpaw for a new television for the family. Reluctant at first to add anything to the household that would incur additional electricity and expense, Granny and Grandpaw finally relented and bought the modern device. Overcome with enthusiasm, the kids found just the perfect spot for their impressive piece of furniture in the sittin' room. Walt Disney movies became Mercy's favorite. Grandpaw's favorite shows were *Amos & Andy* and the local news.

Mercy could not grasp the significance of watching David Brinkley on a daily basis, but then she saw her grandpaw as strange anyway. Later, she would remember how he smiled and actually laughed for the first time watching the *Amos & Andy* show.

TVs are amazin' things, ain't they? They can even make Grandpaw crack a smile.

~~~

During the year, Mercy's uncle Armster (nicknamed Puny) moved into the milk house. He was a tiny man; that's why they called him Puny.

Funny name, but it makes good sense to me. I reckon he's seein' hard times and jist needs a place to stay.

Located beside the main house, the milk house was a place her granny had used for keeping the family's milk and butter cool before the modern conveniences of electricity and refrigerators. A dilapidated wooden structure, it was later used for storing various sized canning jars and a collection of farm tools. It was a simple building, a single room with two narrow, concrete troughs lining the walls that had been used for storing crocks of milk.

Mercy and her brothers watched as Uncle Puny lined the milk house walls with cardboard boxes to insulate it and cover the cracks. He placed a bed and mismatched, leftover furniture pieces inside his tiny home.

Well, I reckon it's nicer 'n my chicken house—but Lordy, not by much!

Mercy couldn't understand *why* Uncle Puny enjoyed living in one room with no running water or electricity. But he often strolled inside the main house to share meals and watch television in the sittin' room. She didn't recall when or why he decided to leave his sanctuary in the milk house, but like all adults, he had a choice about where he lived. Children did not. Instinctively, she knew his stay would not be a lengthy one. No one would stay for very long, she thought, as she mentally compiled the list of Granny's rules in her head.

And Uncle Puny sure didn't.

CHAPTER 17

THE JOT 'EM DOWN STORE

By now, Mercy felt she was mature enough to make a trip by herself to Cleveland. She knew most elderly people did not own cars, a fact which made it difficult for her kinfolk to "trade." They needed basic staples such as sugar, meal, and flour on a regular basis. Musick & Owen's grocery store provided a much-needed service for the most isolated people around Back Valley. Each Saturday morning, a battered Army truck with a green canvas top and sides chugged along Back Valley, Cracker's Neck, and the Weaver's Creek route. Narrow wooden bench seats were fastened in the back of the truck for riders, who could shop in downtown Cleveland while their orders were being filled. The town hardware store, drug store, and bank were businesses essential for everyone, and this weekly opportunity to travel to town was indispensable.

Regularly making use of this free service, Granny carefully prepared her weekly list, marched to the main road, and handed the list to the driver. By mid-afternoon, the driver would appear again, his truck bed filled with boxes of supplies for anyone who had placed an order along the route. An itemized bill was included, and customers typically paid on the spot. Mercy thought charge accounts were allowed, but doubted her granny ever charged anything—at least not for very long.

Riding to Cleveland in the back of that old Army truck became an obsession to Mercy. She thought it would be fascinating to travel to town, all cozy under the protection of the truck's canvas top, and shop downtown to her heart's content. She had often requested permission, but had not been allowed to venture outside Back Valley. Her brothers had gone in the past, but she supposed it was "unladylike" for her to travel to town alone. Mercy continued to plead, and finally Granny agreed she could shop at the new Jot 'Em Down Store. Mercy had heard about the used clothing store from her cousin Linda Joann, and knew her mother's sister, Mildred, worked there. Located directly beside Musick & Owen's grocery store, it would be safe for her to venture there alone, and knowing her aunt worked there, Mercy felt secure. She hoped her aunt had some news of her mother, Nell.

Excited beyond words, she slept restlessly the night before the trip. Out of bed before the crack of dawn, she prepared herself for the adventure of a lifetime. Ready and waiting with Granny's order, Mercy scampered to the main road and waited for the old Army truck to appear. She heard it first, the steady grind of the gears changing as it topped the hill coming up the river road. It halted in front of her; she stepped to the rear of the truck, climbed the tailgate, and took her place on the narrow wooden seat in the back. She was the first one on the truck that day, and she was pleased with the idea of riding alone. Enjoying the solitude of her own thoughts, she traveled the mountain roads up Weaver's Creek and Cracker's Neck, then onto Sandy Ridge. At each stop, she briefly chatted or waved to neighbors and strangers, reveling in her new independence. Along the way, a couple of other passengers boarded the truck, but preferring her solitude by this time, Mercy passed the remainder of the trip with little conversation. Finally, she arrived at Musick & Owen's store and rushed inside to talk with the owner. Mercy enjoyed chatting with Eloise; she was a kind, friendly woman.

What a pretty woman she is! One of the prettiest women I ever did see.

As if Eloise had read Mercy's thoughts, she leaned forward across the glass candy case and handed Mercy a free piece of barrel-shaped root beer candy.

Placing Granny's order into the palm of Eloise's hand, Mercy said, "Oh, thank ye!" and scampered out the door, down the steps to Main Street, then paused in front of the Jot 'Em Down Store. She remembered someone's recent remark that "the secondhand store is an effort to help the poor in Appalachia." And then she pondered about the recent news and President Johnson's "War on Poverty." Mercy had heard about the president's new plan to "eradicate the poorest of the poor" in the region, and that Appalachia was sometimes called "the forgotten America." She had learned about Project Head Start and the Appalachian Regional Commission.

What were they all talkin' about? What's a third-world country? And what war? Russell County's on the list—what list?

What's all that mean? I know I live in the Appalachian Mountains, but surely they ain't talkin' about my area? They must be talkin' about that town *of Appalachia. Yeah, that's probably it... just the town named Appalachia. And what does that have to do with this Jot 'Em Down Store in Cleveland? I don't' know exactly where that town of Appalachia is, but I reckon it's over yonder near Big Stone Gap. It ain't far from where I live, but I sure feel sorry for them poor families in that little town of Appalachia. Well, I'm sure grateful I ain't that poor.*

With all that in mind, Mercy entered the Jot 'Em Down Store. She wasn't especially proud to be purchasing second-hand clothing, but curiosity got the best of her. Everyone was bragging about the new store in town, and she wanted to see what was so special about it. *Cling-a-ling,* the door opened, then closed, and she saw her mother's sister. With her back to the door, Aunt Mildred ignored the bell and stood carefully separating and folding clothing. Rows of blouses, shirts, pants, and skirts were laid out on tables in the center of the room. Dresses, jackets, and coats hung on racks lining each wall. Mercy thought it was a drab looking store. Dimly lit, it lacked the appeal of the front display windows she was used to seeing at Jessee's Mercantile. Rows of strange looking shoes and boots were arranged haphazardly about the room.

Aware she was in the store, her Aunt Mildred came to greet her with open arms. Curious, she searched her aunt's face to discern any likeness to her mother's face. She couldn't be certain. It had been too long, and the seldom-glimpsed photo in the good room had begun to fade, as had her memories. She loved her Aunt Mildred, and recollections of time spent with Linda Joann at her home raced through her mind: how her cousin, Carl, had taught them the art of chewing and spitting tobacco in the backyard; how they had learned to hop across the rocks into the shallow parts of the Clinch River near their backyard; and how she had watched the family restore their home after the 1957 flood.

She knew her aunt had been saddened when Nell had returned and taken baby Randy from their home. Their family had loved and cared for him as if he had been their own, but after more than a year, Nell snatched him from their lives. Mercy knew it had caused a rift between the two sisters. Mercy and Aunt Mildred briefly chatted about the weather, and Mercy began browsing through the piles of clothes, eventually spotting something she liked.

What a bargain, twenty-five cents for a jacket!

The camel-colored blazer perfectly outlined her upper body. The front pocket was missing the popular crown insignia, but she was certain she would find one later. Her Aunt Reatha could sew it on for her. Remembering the traveling dry cleaner truck that made a journey through Back Valley each week, Mercy planned to have it cleaned. Then she would be the proud owner of a nice blazer, just like the other well-dressed girls at school. No one would be the wiser if she didn't divulge to them it had come from the Jot 'Em Down Store. Mercy carried her blazer to the cash register and paid her Aunt Mildred 25 cents. As she turned to leave, she remembered to ask about her mother. By this time, it had been seven years since she had seen her. As usual, there was no news.

Cling-a-ling. She slipped quickly from the store and onto the main sidewalk. Hoping no one had seen her enter or leave the store on Main Street, she carried the brown paper bag with her secret contents tucked neatly inside.

Mercy wanted to see everything Cleveland had to offer that day. Proudly walking across Main Street, she followed the cracked sidewalk to Fraley's Hardware Store. Briefly stepping inside the double doors, she peeked at the rows of games, then the farm tools, and left. Glancing in both directions, she crossed the old train tracks and stared at the rundown train station.

How sad, nobody uses it anymore.

She tried to remember the train trip she had made from that station as a young girl holding tightly to her mother's hand. Flashes of tall field grasses, massive hills, flowing water, and a pale blue sky were all her mind could call up. No other specific details of that train ride to Bluefield, WV came to her. Dismissing these thoughts, Mercy visited Price's Drug Store and the post office. Satisfied that she had savored everything there was to see downtown, she retraced her steps back to Musick & Owen's grocery store for her trip home.

In the old Army truck on her way home to Back Valley, Mercy looked around as if really seeing her mountains for the first time. She realized that her heart belonged here. This place and these mountains nurtured her body and sustained her soul. She loved the sense of security and trusted neighbors, and being able to retire at night with unlocked doors. From these neighbors, she had learned of the important things in life: home, family, church, and place—the abiding mountains. She could not imagine living anywhere else.

She never dreamed this stability and way of life would soon be altered once more.

Excerpt From "Wishes for a Little Girl"
Ella Wheeler Wilcox

But make her fair and comely to the sight,
Give her more heart than brain, more love than pride,
Let her be tender-thoughted, cheerful, bright,
Some strong man's star and guide.
Not vainly questioning why she was sent
Into this restless world of toil and strife,
Let her go bravely on her way, content
To make the best of life.

CHAPTER 18

LIVIN' UP NORTH

A year later, Mercy sat staring into space in a tiny kitchen, day-dreaming about her beloved mountains and wondering why she was now living just outside Detroit. She was no longer in Back Valley, but at 964 West Brickley Avenue, one mile from the busy intersection of Dequindre and Seven Mile Road. The house sat on an unassuming street where multiple identical cookie-cutter homes had been built. There were rows and rows of small, two-story structures, street after street, all built with detached garages and surrounded by well-defined fences. Each structure had a tiny tract of land, no bigger than the barnyard back home in the mountains. Each street honored some type of tree that most people in the city had never seen: Elm, Hickory, Laurel, Oak…

Shucks! City people wouldn't be able to tell one tree from 'nother.

She had been gone from the mountains almost a year now, and much had changed within her. Mercy could clearly remember the conversation with her daddy that eventful day on the telephone. It had been that unexpected, long-distance call from Michigan that led to the chain of events resulting in her eventual move from Back Valley

"Y'all have a new mother," said her daddy

Mercy yelled at her brothers across the room. "What? We have a new mother?! Hooray!"

I couldn't be happier. Maybe now I'll have a real *mother. I'm finally gonna be loved—finally. Besides, Nell's been gone eight years now, and I reckon it's time for all of us to get on with our lives*, Mercy had thought at the time.

And so, Mercy and her brothers moved to the land of milk and honey to begin their new lives, in a little suburb outside Detroit City—not the *city of* Detroit, but Dee-troit *City*. Mercy had never seen so many cars or lanes of traffic as she did during the long drive up I-75. She silently counted eight lanes from the backseat of the car just as they entered the outskirts of Detroit. Cars whizzed everywhere, drivers quickly passing others ahead of them, weaving in and out sporadically. She felt lost.

Why, there's even a minimum *speed limit on this highway! Who ever thought of an idea like that?*

What a departure from Back Valley, where, in most places, there had been just enough roadway for a single car. And courteous drivers pulled to the side of the road to allow an oncoming car to pass. Most of all, she remembered the friendly waves as the drivers came by. She missed that simple gesture most of all, that slight tilt of the fingers from atop the steering wheel, sometimes accompanied with a smile.

But she would adjust, just as she had in the past, to this new change in her life. And so, with a mixture of both enthusiasm and panic, she pushed all her insecurities to the outermost recesses of her mind. The country girl had moved to the city.

"Hillbilly!" Everywhere she had traveled this past year, she heard that word on a daily basis. In the stores, restaurants, parks, and school, it was always there. The word itself did not bother her a great deal. It was the stigma attached to the word that bothered her.

Mercy understood now. As if she stood on the outside peering through a smudged windowpane, she finally saw it clearly. It was not just the *town* of Appalachia that was included in that famous declaration of war on poverty. LBJ's War on Poverty encompassed *her* place of birth, *her* beloved home in Back Valley, and *her* beautiful mountains.

Mercy felt dejected, deprived, and embarrassed as she struggled with deep shame brought on by hearing that single word, *hillbilly.* She was conflicted in her thoughts of how to deal with the insensitivity of others. Everyone up North, the "Yankees," seemed to enjoy using that hated name to describe her Appalachian drawl and make demeaning jokes about her place of birth.

Oh boy, I'm sure glad they don't know 'bout me bein' born in Uncle Taze's truck. They'd have a real laugh 'bout that! Or that my mother's real name is Nell—Nell Head. I've had too many kids laugh at my mother's name. I can still hear their voices ringin' in my ears...Nail Head, Nail Head, Nail Head.

More persistent and strong-willed than ever before, Mercy dug in her heels, smiled often, and learned to laugh *with* them. "Hold that chin up," she recalled someone telling her...and she had. She often reminded herself she had been through tougher times.

As if telepathically putting a halt to Mercy's newest train of thought, Mary walked into the kitchen, jolting Mercy's thoughts back to the present. She'd enjoyed being alone and now resented her stepmother's intrusion. But without a word, Mercy closed her math book and quietly watched her stepmother as she rushed to prepare dinner for the brood.

Another meal of that Gawd-awful Yankee dish: goulash, they call it. Mixed with all them strange things. Why, no person in their right mind would eat that shit and like it! But I been trained a long time ago not to complain about vittles, and to eat whut's placed in front o' me.

Mercy gawked at her stepmother. Really stared at her for a long time. Almost six feet tall and with short-cropped, coal-black hair, Mary didn't look like a lady at all. Larger framed than the average female, her oversized breasts jutted forward in her blouse like rockets ready for lift-off. Mercy knew her stepmother had dyed her hair days earlier, but the solution, in spite of everything she'd tried, continued to stain her scalp. Like a black swimmer's cap, the dye outlined the sides of her face and ears. Thick red lipstick had been smeared on her tiny lips.

Yeah, that's it. I ain't sure Mary is a lady: you know, a real woman. She looks like a clown—a male clown.

The sides of Mercy's mouth turned slightly upward, and she smiled at the thought. Just a hint of a smile, just in case her stepmother sensed she was being observed.

Wonder what Daddy sees in her? Ain't a bit purty, ain't a bit womanly, ain't a bit nothin'!

Mary dropped noodles into her strange concoction, still unaware she was being scrutinized from the little hidey-hole in the corner of the kitchen.

Somehow reminds you of a witch makin' a brew. That's

it! I believe I jist discovered a new name for my stepmother: the Stepwitch. Stepwitch! Stepwitch! Stepwitch! Kinda makes me feel a lil' bit like Cinderella.

Slipping silently out of the hidey-hole, Mercy gingerly tiptoed to the basement, all without being seen. She enjoyed the solitude of the makeshift room in the basement, where she could be alone to continue her thoughts.

The stepwitch had two sons from a previous marriage, and she and her brothers added to the brood of five children. From time to time, Mercy felt overwhelmed with living in a family of four boys, but she had become skilled at adapting to new situations—and learning from boys. By now, she had learned baseball, softball, basketball, ice skating, and the art of chewing and spitting tobacco.

Most of all, Mercy reveled in full use of the bathroom and *real* toilet paper.

No more corncobs, or Sears and Roebuck catalogues, or newspapers, but real paper that feels soft on your hind end. Maybe that's where people get that old sayin': "she acts likes she's got a corn cob stuck up her ass."

But after discovering how much toilet paper had been used, the stepwitch began locking it up and rationing it out.

"Why'd you lock the toilet paper up?" asked Mercy

"Too many asses in this family!" Mary flatly stated.

The stepwitch had an entire vocabulary of words Mercy had never heard. *Queer, prick, fag,* and lots more words spewed like a geyser from her mouth on a regular basis.

Oh, if only Preacher Kiser from back home could hear all them bad words! Lord A 'Mercy on her poor soul!

Most of the time, her daddy's and Mary's bedroom was locked and placed off limits to the children, but Mercy didn't mind. She had grown accustomed to locked rooms and closets, and the rationing mentality of her granny.

~~~

That year, Mercy began eighth grade in a city school. The most stunning surprise was when she discovered there were no school buses, just city transportation. Walking to the bus stop and boarding the city bus was a scary experience for a mountain girl. An even bigger revelation was that it cost 25 cents to ride.

Each morning as she boarded the bus, she stuck her quarter in the slot and edged her way to a seat far from strange-looking passengers. Uneasy around the adult passengers, Mercy remained guarded against any potentially dangerous situation. Every now and then, she chose to walk the mile to school rather than part with her quarter. She preferred saving the change and stopping by the store for a sweet treat on her way home in the afternoons.

It was on the city bus that she met her first challenge in Detroit. Mercy overheard a friend being teased and ridiculed by a gang of girls almost every day. One day, just as her friend began to cry, Mercy decided it was the moment to intervene. It was time to stop the bullying. She did it the only way she knew how; her balled-up fist met the bully's eye. Mercy and the bully tumbled into the center aisle of the bus, fighting like many girls, yelling, scratching, and pulling hair. Ignoring the commotion, the city bus driver simply continued his route. Mercy had made her first stand; there would be no further teasing from the city girls. Her brothers had trained her well, and she had discovered a valuable lesson: she must stand up for herself—and others, when necessary. She would never accept being bullied.

In time, Mercy learned a new, more popular song. She had grown tired of her old song, "Wolverton Mountain." Her new favorite was "Last Night I Went to Sleep in Dee-troit City." Each night, she sang the words and wept for her relatives and friends back home. By the end of the school year, she was anxious to return to her friends and the familiar surroundings in Back Valley.

All in all, she had enjoyed the new school and her busy neighborhood, but she longed for the peace and comfort of the mountains. Her memories of brilliant-hued sunsets, the freshness of the mountain air, and the stillness of the summer's nights called to her.

And once again, she had not felt loved. In addition, Mercy had not liked the bickering—the arguing between her daddy and stepmother about...the children...your children...my children. Mercy had seen the favoritism her stepmother had lavished upon her own two children. She told herself she could deal with that. By now, she had grown accustomed to the fact that not all children were loved equally. As sure as she could be of anything in life, Mercy was certain of that. Her experiences with Granny had taught her many things, but that most of all.

Mercy watched her daddy work tirelessly throughout the week and witnessed his pattern of drinking escalate by Friday afternoon. It was a consistent ritual—work all week, drink all weekend. Sometimes Mercy's stepmother would join him in drinking at nearby bars. More often than not when they returned home, they argued late into the night. As her daddy's drunken temper overtook him, arguments often escalated into full-blown fights. She didn't enjoy witnessing her daddy's drunken wrath every weekend.

In the past, Mercy had seen her daddy's brutal attacks on her stepmother. She had seen him hit her with balled-up fists—and watched blood run out of the corners of her eyes. Over time, all the kids had been conditioned to stay out of the way when he was drinking, and simply retreated to their rooms.

Occasionally, the stepwitch raced upstairs to warn them. "You guys need to stay in your rooms. Don't come down here now, so hide, your daddy is crazy drunk tonight!" And off she would scamper back down the steps, attempting to calm him before he could wreak havoc on the entire house. Mercy dreaded those times the most. She had hidden in her closet one too many times, and now thought it best to return to Back Valley—even in spite of her granny's rules.

There's no love in this home, neither. Let LBJ declare war on poverty in Appalachia. But I'm goin' home to Back Valley.

Before the end of the school year, Mercy dialed her granny's long-distance number.

"Granny, I jist wanna come home. I don't like livin' up here in this big city. I wanna come back to the mountains, back to my friends."

Without taking the time to think about the request, Granny said, "Now you know you don't mind me; you're too sassy. I can't have it. I won't have it."

Mercy had already prepared herself for that comment. She pleaded, "But Granny, please, I'm homesick. I don't like the schools here, and the girl gangs and them city buses, they're scary. I'll mind from now on. I promise I will, I promise I won't be sassy."

After a long pause, Granny said, "Well, I'll think about it, I reckon. Remember, you'd have to mind and not be sassy. I could still send you to that orphanage in Grundy!"

Mercy had promised with her fingers crossed behind her back.

After much thought, Gary Wayne and Darrell decided not to return to the mountains with Mercy.

I'll sure miss 'em, both of 'em—mostly Gary Wayne, but even Darrell, some.

Once again, R.C. drove Mercy back to her mountains.

During their visit, Granny allowed R.C. and Mary to sleep in her good room, along with Mary's six-year-old son, Randy. After a short stay, they returned to the city, going back up North, leaving Mercy behind.

Oh, Lord A' mercy! Granny found out Randy pissed in her bed, right there in the good room!

And Mercy smiled as she thought about the hissy fit Granny threw after they left.

CHAPTER 19

BLOOD KIN

The autumn sun shone from the brilliant sky above, highlighting the red and yellow maples on the hillsides. Mercy lifted her face, capturing the last remnants of the afternoon sun, staring at her mountains. She was home again.

It felt good to be home again, among her blood kin; Mercy was impatient to see all of them. She decided to spend her first afternoon visiting nearby relatives. She wanted to see her cousin Bobbie first. Aunt Lill and Uncle Doc's place lay a short distance through the field from Granny's house. A well-worn narrow path lined with tall weeds and poison ivy led straight to their property line. She loved that old path, enjoyed the solitude and peaceful feeling it gave her as it meandered its way across the open field. She knew her kinfolk often used the path as a shortcut for their frequent trips to Artrip to buy pop and Vienna sausages. Excitedly, she crossed the fence, hopped down the rickety wooden steps, and sauntered by the old barn and toilet. The old outhouse brought back earlier memories; it was here she had puffed on her first Pall Mall cigarette. Eager to be daring, Mercy and Bobbie had snatched her uncle's cigarettes, run into the toilet, and puffed away. Nothing exciting about cigarettes, they decided, and threw them down the hole so no one would find them. Petrified at being caught, they had not realized the smoke had streamed out through the cracks for everyone to see. Mercy laughed out loud at herself while strolling into Aunt Lill's side yard.

Lucky we weren't caught, or we both might've been switched! Sure glad nobody was around to see that smoke comin' through the cracks in that outhouse.

Carefully stepping around the cement ditch, she climbed the rock steps onto the porch and crossed the threshold into the kitchen. Mercy knew it was unnecessary to knock; all she had to do was just holler. Family was always welcome.

That's the way it is with blood kin.

Aunt Lill, already busy with the evening's supper, stopped to greet her. They hugged and Mercy asked about Bobbie. They had always been close cousins, and she longed to see her.

"She ain't here, but she'll be back dreckly. You want a drink o' water?" Aunt Lill asked, pointing toward the bucket and dipper beside the door.

Mercy knew it was a simple mountain courtesy to offer water to visitors. And Aunt Lill and Uncle Doc's water was considered the best around: the only open hand-dug well still used in these parts, she remembered. An old wooden bucket attached to a rope was still used to draw up the fresh, sparkling water. All guests were expected to at least sip the water; it was considered impolite not to do so. Mercy dipped the long dipper into the bucket, all the way down, and raised it to her lips.

That's the best tastin', coldest water I ever had.

Aunt Lill's stooped shoulders and rounded spine gave evidence of the hard life she had lived—raising nine children, tending a garden patch, preserving food, working tobacco, and carrying wood and coal for the house fires. Mercy watched her prepare the table for supper. She never understood why Aunt Lill always kept the table completely set, bowls and plates turned upside down, silverware tucked neatly beside each dish. Now, Aunt Lill turned the plates and bowls upward. Saying her goodbyes, Mercy stepped out the door, spoke to her cousins Jen and Hawk sitting on the porch, and retraced her steps back to the path.

She wanted to visit her cousin Sylvie, but decided to gather chinquapins first. She loved the sweetness of the tiny chestnuts, but the dwarf bushes had become harder to find through the years. Aunt Lill and Uncle Doc's property ran alongside the main road; Mercy knew a few chinquapin bushes might still remain on the hill across the road. It was there she had patiently gathered the nuts in years past. She hoped they had not died, like all the other bushes, while she had been living in Michigan. With this change in plans, she backtracked along the path, climbed the steep hill, crossed the split rail fence, and jumped onto the paved highway.

With familiarity and a sense of confidence, Mercy scarcely slowed her pace as she crossed the narrow road. She knew few cars traveled the back roads here, unlike the busy city streets of Detroit.

It's sure nice walkin' on this smooth pavement. Nothin' like the streets in Dee-troit, but jist as nice. I sure don't miss that constant buzzin' of traffic and horns honkin' up there, on them busy city streets.

Mercy took notice that the old persimmon tree, its branches laden with fruit, still welcomed travelers at the bend in the curve. She chose not to try the persimmons again.

I didn't like 'em before, probably still don't like 'em. Them things will pucker your mouth for sure.

Her pace quickened as she readied herself for the stiff climb up the hill to the chinquapin patch. The few remaining bushes were loaded with the prickly burrs this year. From past experience, she remembered how hard it was to remove the spiny burrs; it was better to wait until they had begun to open. She pulled her shirt-sleeves forward to protect her hands and carefully plucked the tiny spheres from the bush. Satisfied she had collected enough, she loaded the newly picked chinquapins into the tail of her shirt and eased down the hill. Running to Granny's house, she dumped her prize into a pail. She would return later to shell them.

By now it was late afternoon, and Mercy still wanted to visit her cousin. She had wasted precious daylight hours. Remembering her granny's early bedtime rule, she knew her visit with Sylvie would be a short one.

Mercy almost always ran everywhere she went throughout the valley. Today was no different. She sprinted to the graveled road in front of her granny's house, puffed up the hill at the forks of the road, and turned toward Sylvie's. With renewed enthusiasm and appreciation for her beloved home in the valley, she paused again to soak in the beauty of golden hickory leaves and the green of the mountain laurel. Summer had lingered this year into September, with warmer nights and longer than usual fall afternoons.

It sure is beautiful here in the mountains.

It was an easy jog, only about a half-mile to her cousin's home. Mercy had not talked to Sylvie since she had left Back Valley, so she was eager to hear the latest news. Sylvie lived with her four sons, Monroe, Glen, and the identical twins, Ronald and Donald. Mercy reminded herself to try to remember which twin was which this time.

Over the years, I've always had trouble tellin' 'em apart, 'specially when they're not standin' or sittin' side by side. Maybe I'll be lucky this time, and they'll be on the porch, sittin' in the swing. I'll have a much better chance of catchin' Donald's gabbiness to compare with Ronald's quiet-like nature.

From the front porch, perched in her favorite homemade rocker, Sylvie had seen Mercy approach. As expected, Sylvie offered her the customary drink of water—and an apple. The family owned a small apple orchard that always had the best tasting fruit, Mercy remembered.

I'll have both, the apple and the water.

"How ye been?" Sylvie asked, just as she tucked the final dip of snuff way back inside her mouth. The remnants of the last snuff slowly trickled from the corner of her mouth, outlining the creases in her ancient face.

Sylvie spread out her arms, "Come and gimme a big hug."

"I'm good now. How're you guys?" Mercy responded just as the twins stepped from the living room onto the porch.

Now, which twin is which?

Just as she expected, they both settled into the swing opposite Mercy's rocker; she'd be careful how she addressed them. She never wanted them to know that after all these years; she *still* didn't know who was who.

They noticed at once she had acquired that Yankee accent and vocabulary, saying "you guys," not "y'all."

I'll have to quit that. People somehow don't take to that here in the valley; they'll be callin' me a ferriner pretty soon.

"Ye talk funny now," Sylvie said and picked up another tad of snuff to tuck even farther back in her mouth.

"Yeah, I know; I can't seem to help it." Mercy responded, all the while trying to put a little twang back into her speech so they wouldn't be offended by her newfound Yankee dialect. Recalling how difficult it had been to survive the hillbilly comments in Michigan, Mercy didn't want people laughing at her accent—not again.

I'll have to work hard to fit back in again around these parts.

Catching up on the latest family and community news, Mercy promised to return soon for another visit. Before she left, Sylvie led her to the pantry under the high front porch. Rows upon rows of canned goods sat atop wooden shelves that ran the full length of the room. Reaching way in the back past the peaches, green beans, and kraut, Sylvie pulled out a can of prize-winning pickled beets. Everyone knew Mercy loved home-canned food, and Sylvie always shared her best with her. Mercy happily accepted the gift, and promised to eat the pickled beets with her next bowl of soup beans and corn bread. Saying goodbye, she turned her face homeward, taking care to keep the canned beets safe. Mercy's breathing slowed, her pace slowed...even her thoughts slowed, giving her time to enjoy the return to her mountains.

CHAPTER 20

HOME AGAIN

As usual, Granny and Grandpaw went to bed with the chickens. Mercy found it hard to go to bed before sunset again, but she knew her granny's views on bedtime would never change; she was too old and set in her ways. Mercy had at least finally convinced her granny she was too old to sleep with her anymore.

Besides, I'm in ninth grade now! And I'm tired of Granny tellin' me to hursh and go to sleep!

Mercy was given her brothers' bed in the sitting room.

A bed of my own at Granny's! I never thought I'd see the day!

Mercy was busier than ever, with even more chores on the farm now. With both her brothers gone, she was the only one left to help her grandparents. The endless chopping of wood, hauling in coal, slopping hogs, gathering eggs, and washing dishes were all-consuming.

But it's better than livin' in the city and dealin' with the step-witch and daddy's drinkin'. Anythin' is better than that.

Mercy learned to coax the cows home for morning and after-noon milkings. "Swuck…swuck…swuck," she'd call. She grew adept at following the cow paths around the side of the hill, some-times even before daylight. Granny kept insisting Mercy learn to milk the cows—but Mercy stubbornly refused. Throughout the years, she had watched cows being milked, and she was horrified at the possibility of being kicked. She promised herself she would not add this frightening chore to her already hectic day.

She recalled a story someone had once shared about her mother that did nothing to change her mind. Nell had been scared of ornery cows, too, and had resisted R.C.'s demands that she learn the art of milking. In fact, on one occasion, when she had stubbornly refused to milk, R.C. had beaten Nell with his belt—his method of punishing her for disobedience.

Although Granny was furious with her and scolded her for being lazy, Mercy steadfastly refused to budge.

Besides, I like knowin' I might be a little bit like my mommy.

Mercy thought about another battle when she had refused to help her granny. Years before, she had been ordered to kill a chicken and prepare it for Sunday dinner. Watching her granny grab the chickens, drag them to the chopping block, and cut off their heads had horrified her. Standing at the chopping block, axe in hand, Mercy simply froze; she couldn't chop off that poor crit-ter's head! Although she had seen chickens lose their heads in the past, knowing their anguish was prolonged as they flopped around headless had disgusted her. She wouldn't do it. She *couldn't* do it. She cried at the prospect of causing so much pain to an innocent critter. Eventually, Granny gave up her struggle to force Mercy to kill a chicken, and Mercy smiled at the thought of winning another battle with Granny.

~~~

During that year, her grandpaw was diagnosed with the dreaded coal miner's Black Lung disease. Mercy had mixed emotions the day the large oxygen tank was delivered to their home and placed by his bedside in the sittin' room. She had watched his health decline over the past couple of years, but with little emotion. His severe coughing had increased, and he spat black-coated phlegm on a daily basis. Mercy hated hearing his incessant coughing, detested watching him spit into the fireplace.

Why can't I feel somethin'? Is it because I'm ungrateful? What's wrong with me? Why is it impossible to feel sorry for 'im? I reckon it's because he's been so mean to me through the years. His quick temper, them harsh whuppins, his angry words. Him tellin' me to cry in a cry pie when I was little. He never showed me, not once, that he loved me. He never said the words "I love you." Neither did Granny. Maybe Grandpaw loved me in his own way, but I can't forgive him. I won't forget the times he picked me up and beat the livin' daylights out of me. And I ain't gonna forget when he threw logs and hammers at us, neither. Or the times he raised tobacco sticks and cane switches to us, and made my legs bleed. I reckon I probably deserved that paddlin' I got playin' with the gravels in the headlane when I was five, cuz it was a dangerous place and I'm lucky a car didn't hit me. I deserved that one, I reckon. But beyond that, I got more 'n my fair share of paddlins from both Grandpaw and Granny. But I know I ain't been treated no different than Grandpaw treated all his chil-

*dren before me, especially the girls. I heard all them stories about
beatins he gave my aunts and uncles. Maybe because they're older now, with children of their own...well, maybe they've forgiven
Grandpaw, but I won't. I don't feel no sympathy for him. And I
don't feel guilty.*

Mercy had come to the conclusion early on that boys played
more important roles in families, sometimes helping to disci-
pline their younger sisters. Her brother, Darrell, enjoyed that
role. Girls, simply by their gender and the fate they were dealt,
were viewed as inferior, insignificant contributors in the families.
Mercy didn't appreciate the hierarchy position men enjoyed in
the mountains. She recalled how when at large family gatherings,
men ate first at the dinner table, then the women, and then the
children. She had stubbornly questioned that tradition time and
again, but had been quickly silenced by her granny. "Men just do!
That's the way it is. Men just do!" Granny had responded, obviously content with her station in life.

*I get tired of watchin' all them big men eat, then waitin' for
the women to finish, and finally eatin' cold leftovers. A kid could
starve to death waitin' around here. I'll never understand that
rule, no matter how hard they try explainin' it to me. Educatin'
girls ain't important cuz they're expected to get married, settle
down, and have lots of babies. Just like the third-world mentality
LBJ talked about on the news. Maybe there really is somethin' to
all this War on Poverty.*

"Much needed to be accomplished to break the chain," she
remembered hearing David Brinkley say. Mercy loved school and
very early on, she sensed the importance of an education; she
vowed to break the chain within her family. She knew her father
had not graduated from school, nor had most of her aunts and uncles. They were encouraged to drop out and help with the never-

ending chores on the tobacco farm. Luckily, her Aunt Reatha and Uncle Denver persevered and graduated, even attending college for a while. Her Uncle Denver had once taught in the one-room schoolhouse on Weaver's Creek.

I think I might like that, to be a teacher.

Perhaps her grandparents' attitudes had been molded in their own formative years, but societal expectations were changing, Mercy sensed. It was the mid-1960s: the era of the mini-skirt, the hippie movement, and other radical changes. Change was coming, even to the mountains.

Whether they like it or not.

CHAPTER 21

RAGGIN' IT

Weary of the winter's chill, the yellow Easter lilies, purple crocuses, and white snowballs sought comfort and warmth from the sun as they pushed to the surface. An unseen hand splashed color haphazardly across the mountain landscape. A sense of rebirth and newness permeated the air.

As spring burst forth, so did Mercy's body. She had already experienced her dreaded "monthly" for the first time while living in Michigan, but now she was reluctant to share that secret with her granny. Mercy was frustrated with the inevitability, the inescapability of her preparation for womanhood. Her budding breasts, tender from constant rubbing against her clothing, had forewarned her of physical changes yet to come.

But how can I tell Granny? I need supplies, things the step-witch bought me while I was livin' in Michigan, things I been secretly buyin' with the hidden money from Uncle Lawrence. Girl things—Modess pads, just another ridiculous thing for girls to put up with! Why not boys instead?! Why can't they have somethin' stuck between their legs every month? Just another reason boys are so lucky.

And she sulked because of the unfairness of the situation.

Scurrying to the outhouse to hide the latest monthly evidence, Mercy knew it was time to ask for money to buy Modess Pads. It would be a subject not easily discussed; she reasoned it was likely to be a secret, a family secret. She recognized her granny would rebuff any attempt to discuss the female menstrual cycle. She planned to wait until the afternoon, a time of relaxation, when her granny would be rocking on the front porch. Granny would be more approachable, less critical—she hoped. Mercy's mind whirled with ways to approach her granny, not an easy task—especially when it was about money, and personal things. Most of all, she reminded herself not to be sassy.

Late that afternoon, Mercy scurried to perch herself on the porch swing, positioning her body for the most favorable view of any car that might pass the main road. She never wanted to miss a single car; it gave her pleasure to wave to each driver as they passed. And Granny, already seated near the end of the porch, moved to and fro in her favorite rocking chair.

Reasoning there was no correct way to approach delicate matters, and without further thoughts of retribution, Mercy calmly asked, "Granny, did you ever kiss Grandpaw before you married him?"

Visibly caught off guard, Granny's rocking movements abruptly halted. Leaning forward in the chair with her hands gripping the rocker arms tightly and her feet firmly planted, her face paled; dark Indian eyes blackened as she sought Mercy's gaze.

She responded in a huff, "Why, people don't talk about stuff like that!" The rhythm of the rocking chair resumed, a movement Mercy knew meant dismissal.

"Well, why not?"

"'Cause they ain't supposed to, that's all. It ain't proper, it ain't womanlike!"

Intent on not letting the conversation end, Mercy asked again, "Well, did you kiss him at least *once* before you married him?"

"Hursh, I said I ain't talkin' about it. Now go on. Find somethin' to keep you busy. Grab a broom; the floor needs cleanin'. Now go!" She pointed in the direction of the broom, deftly sweeping her aged fingers upward to straighten the diaper on her head, then downward to secure the diaper knot at the base. This was a signal of caution and a warning to Mercy, familiar body language that indicated further discussion on this topic would not be tolerated.

Grabbing the broom handle, Mercy inched its tiny bristles into the cracks of the pine wood, back and forth, back and forth, until she swept away the last remnants of the winter's coal dust from the porch. Then she picked her teeth with a bristle from the upper part of the broom handle.

But what'll I use? What'll I do? I ain't got no more sanitary napkins. And Granny has to know by now! Don't she?

Convinced her granny likely already knew or at least suspected her monthly, Mercy simply blurted out, "Granny, I need some Modess pads!"

Finally, her secret was revealed.

Not skipping a beat, the porch rocker continued.

"Well, I ain't got no money for such things; them things cost too much!"

Frustrated with the long wait to discuss her plight, Mercy pleaded, "Granny, I've started my monthly and I need somethin' to wear!"

"Well, you'll just have to do what other women did."

"And what's that?"

"Make 'em outa rags."

"Rags! I ain't goin' to school wearin' no disgustin' rags!"

But she did.

Finding rags was easy, since few cloth items were ever wasted in the family. They were used to bind sores or wounds, and to hold poultices on chests during colds. Worn-out sheets, wash cloths, towels, and chop sack materials were all used for different purposes around the farm. Rags were plentiful.

Month after month, Mercy learned the art of stripping sheets into rows, cutting them into smaller strips, folding them neatly in the shape of sanitary napkins, and then carefully positioning them in place with a safety pin.

But the embarrassment! The embarrassment if anyone should find out haunted her.

Why, what would happen if one of them things fell out at school! I'd die. I'd die! I know I'd die! Jist as sure as if I stuck a gun to my head, I'd be dead!

Mercy prided herself on her clean clothes and shoes, even if they were from the Jot 'Em Down Store. She prided herself on staying neat and keeping her hair clean, even though she had long since stopped using homemade lye soap. Uncle Lawrence provided shampoos, toothpaste, soaps, and deodorant for her use. As was his habit, he brought bags of leftover, half-used bottles of shampoos, old squeezed tubes of toothpaste, and different brands of deodorant during his visits throughout the year. His deliveries provided Mercy with the personal hygiene products she needed. She was grateful for Uncle Lawrence's throwaways.

But I've had enough of them rags! Plenty enough!

She devised a plan that would take place at school the next day.

Raising her hand, Mercy said, "Mrs. Yates, can I be excused?"

"*May* I be excused, not *can* I be excused," said Mrs. Yates in her most formal teacher voice.

"Oh yeah, *may* I?" Mercy responded, eager to please her teacher.

Darn teachers can be so frustratin'! That teacher probably knows I got a rag stuck between my legs, and is jist torturin' me.

"And for what?" Mrs. Yates questioned.

"Ah, I need to go to the bathroom," Mercy lied.

"OK, but be back in time for the test in five minutes." She was dismissed.

Remembering not to run in the hallway, Mercy dashed to the main office, where she knew the treasure she needed would be found. A full stock of sanitary pads was always kept in the office for emergency situations; any girl could request a pad at school.

As she walked into the main office, she caught sight of parents waiting to speak to the principal, students requesting late passes, and teachers roaming to and fro. With eyes downcast, feet shuffling, she moved toward the counter, hoping to escape any chance of eye contact with anyone.

Oh, Lord, have mercy on me! Don't let 'em ask what I'm doin' here before I can get to Miss Dotson.

The school secretary, Rosemary Dotson, was a young woman whom Mercy found to be consistently kind. And most importantly, she would ask few questions. Praying no one would overhear her, especially any male teacher, Mercy whispered, "Miss Dotson, I need a pad. I just started, you know, this morning, after I got to school." (She was careful to add the "after I got to school" part.)

I don't want Miss Dotson to know I can't afford to buy my own. Besides, maybe all the mountain girls do that. Maybe they all lie. Maybe they're all poor jist like me. I hate admittin' I'm poor.

Without question, Miss Dotson reached beneath the counter, leaned inward to scoop up the pad, and handed it to Mercy.

Oh, Lord, don't let her hold that thing up too high. Someone might see it and know what I'm doin'!

Reaching behind the counter, Mercy swept the small box from Miss Dotson's outstretched hand and stuffed it deep into the bottom of her purse, all the while hoping no visitor in the office would be wise to their actions.

Lordy, now I can throw away at least one of them rags. I sure love them new pads, them things are nice! They feel so good. Normal—I feel normal, jist like everybody else. I know all them rich girls don't have to wear them rags and I swanee, I ain't neither, at least not for very long.

Inside the girl's bathroom, she carefully placed the item in the correct position, pinned it down, and scurried back to class.

Jist watch me struttin', struttin' down this hall. Look at me, look at me now. I'm wearin' somethin' new, even if people can't see it. I ain't wearin' no rag, not now. I don't care if everybody in school knows I'm having a period cuz I'm wearin' a new Modess pad stuck between my legs!

Smiling to herself, she walked proudly into the classroom.

Each month that year, Mercy visited Miss Dotson at least once in the main office.

CHAPTER 22

GRAPEVINE ON ORB HILL

School began and Mercy immersed herself in old friends and schoolwork. As always, hours spent at school were her happiest times. Checking books out of the school library on a regular basis, she delved into the mysteries offered by famous authors, and perhaps some not so famous. Any form of literature interested her, it didn't matter; reading was essential. Her ninth grade English teacher, Mrs. Porterfield, encouraged that reading. She offered an incentive for the student who would read the most books throughout the year. Hoping to win this award, Mercy continued reading with renewed fervor.

Winters can be the nastiest of times in the mountains, and yet, the most breathtakingly beautiful. This winter's relentless snow-storms carpeted the surrounding hills and valleys in Weaver's Creek. For weeks, morning's sunrise revealed new visions and wonders to behold. Every snowfall produced virgin snow, each flake settling to rest atop others already there. Mounds of snow grew higher and trees became more obscured with each nightfall. Sub-zero temperatures triggered the formation of huge dripping icicles visible on road banks and the eaves of porches.

Roads became nearly impassable, and a deep sense of solitude spread throughout the valley. Piles of mud-spattered snow lay beside the river road, leftovers from the snowplows sent to clear the mountain roads. Schools were closed for days, sometimes weeks as the winter storms swept through with unparalleled wrath. Tall hemlocks drooped as if weighed down by iron anchors. Too proud to fall, they hung precariously across the roadways. The mountains looked just like a Christmas card, only real.

Standing on the front porch, Mercy reached up, snapped an icicle from its perch, and raised it toward her mouth. She began to reminisce about her brothers. Sucking on the icicle, she thought about a game she'd played with her brothers in earlier years. It had been a test of endurance, an I-dare-you game. She glanced toward the branch that ran beside the bottom property; many winters had been spent playing there, near the ice-covered creek. Mercy and her brothers often cracked the ice, stuck in their bare hands, and competed to see who could endure the cold the longest. It was painful, she remembered. As tough as her brothers had been, she didn't think she had often won that game.

Glancing toward the front lot, Mercy realized again how much she missed Gary Wayne.

The icicle melted quickly in her mouth.

The afternoon sun must be warmin' up things.

Mercy had spent hours playing with her brothers in the snow, at that very place. Smiling, she recalled times spent fashioning snowmen, igloos, and even tunnels. She remembered one specific big snow tunnel. All three had built an L-shaped igloo, carefully packing the frozen, compacted snow into place. Eager to try their new igloo, Mercy had crawled in on hands and knees. It had certainly been a tight fit, she recalled. She had turned and crawled toward the exit, but realized she hadn't been able to get out; her brothers had sealed both ends, and she had been trapped. Mercy had beaten the walls, screamed, yelled and kicked, but to no avail. Certain that Granny and Grandpaw had been unable to hear her screams, she had feared the worst.

Mercy's gut feeling was that her brothers had been teasing, but her breathing had become labored as panic overtook her emotions. Time had stood still, and she had no idea how long she had suffered alone in that space.

I remember thinkin' 'bout how they were gonna find my lifeless body, jist froze right there, what they'd say when lookin' down at me. Maybe, "bless her lil' heart," or "I hope she didn't suffer long," and what final words might be said at my funeral.

But just as she had suspected this was her final breath, the walls cracked and packed snow cascaded in on her; her brothers, laughing like loons, had dug her out. She swore never to crawl into another tunnel—never, ever, not as long as she lived!

By summer, Mercy had forgotten the frightening tunnel experience. She and her brothers had found other ways to entertain themselves. One of their favorite pastimes had been to swing on the grapevine on Orb Hill. They had been warned to stay away from that huge grapevine, but as usual, they did not heed those warnings. They loved passing the time swinging back and forth on the vines across the gully near their home. No one would get hurt, they wouldn't fall; they were invincible, they thought. The three took turns swinging, holding on tight as the tangled vine swooped them from one side of the gully to the other. Mercy estimated it was a good 25-foot drop to the bottom below. But one day, after years of wear and tear, that old grapevine broke. SNAP! Limbs, leaves and vines plummeted into the abyss, and so did Gary Wayne! His yells echoed throughout the valley. Mercy and Darrell clambered down the hill to his side. They tried to keep him quiet, since they knew Granny and Grandpaw would hear his screaming, but Gary Wayne just bellowed louder! They were in a real quandary now. What would they do? How could they tell Granny and Grandpaw they had disobeyed, and now Gary Wayne was hurt? Since they couldn't tell their grandparents how or where the injury had occurred, they planned to lie. Concerned about the repercussions and the whipping they would no doubt receive, they began work on a detailed plan. Soon, they had devised an elaborate scheme.

By this time it was late afternoon, suppertime, and Mercy and Darrell meekly moved toward the family table with Gary Wayne in tow. They had supported their brother down Orb Hill, but now Gary Wayne was on his own to act as if nothing had happened. During the meal, his face turned pasty as he suffered the nearly unbearable pain in his right arm. Unable to eat with his right hand, he scooped food into his mouth with his left. Mercy knew he was in pain. She felt helpless, knowing his hand or arm was likely broken. She wanted to tell the truth, wanted them to know her brother was hurt, but she was too afraid. Since Gary Wayne was normally quiet, Granny and Grandpaw took no note of his strange behavior. Time passed slowly. As soon as they could leave the table, they hurried out to the front lot to put Gary Wayne's plan into motion.

They had decided that during a softball game, he would fall hard, drop on his right arm and "holler until the cows came home."

They had set it up for all to see; everyone would be sitting on the front porch after supper, and so the game began. Shielding his dangling right hand from his grandparents, Gary Wayne swung the bat with his left arm. Toward first base he sprinted and then suddenly tumbled to the ground. Yelling, screaming and flopping, he floundered around like a fish out of water. All the while he was shrieking, "I broke my arm! I broke my arm!"

The scheme worked. Gary Wayne was driven to the hospital, and his broken wrist placed in a cast. No one had been the wiser. Only the kids knew, and it was years before they disclosed to anyone the truth about Gary Wayne's accident.

Mercy chuckled aloud to herself.

I miss my brother Gary Wayne. Will he ever come home again? The land of milk and honey seems so far away.

CHAPTER 23

GRANNY'S DEAD ROOM

Over time, Grandpaw's condition worsened. The Black Lung disease had slowly overpowered his already emaciated body, and he was exhausted from the incessant coughing and spitting. He was admitted into the hospital, and the doctors hinted he might not survive the night. Aunt Reatha and Uncle Paul traveled from Narrows for a brief visit. Granny wanted to visit Grandpaw, so she left with Uncle Paul for the long ride to Lebanon General Hospital. Since she would be gone for a while, Mercy and Aunt Reatha decided to clean the house thoroughly before Granny returned. Mercy and her aunt knew Granny wanted the wake to be held in the home, not at the local funeral parlor. The house was old now and in disrepair, so there was much preparation to be done.

"How can we hold a wake here with everythin' so dusty, so old, so unfancy-like?" Mercy asked, as she glanced about the living room.

Picking up the mop and broom, Aunt Reatha replied, "Oh, we'll jist do the best we can, Mercy honey, the best we can. We jist do what we have to do."

The two decided to clean and rearrange the living room before Granny returned. It was the most likely spot to hold all the company that would be visiting soon. The old floor was sagging, they noted. They worried it could not withstand the weight of a casket, especially with the body in it.

"Why, that casket'll fall right through that floor if we put it there!" Aunt Reatha said, as she pointed toward the far-left corner of the room.

"Lordy, what'll we do? What'll we do?!" said Mercy.

Now, how embarrassin' that would be! I know lots of people will be visitin' soon, and I'd jist die if that casket drops through that floor! I'd die, I'd die, I know I'd die! They'd probably have to put me right up there in that casket beside Grandpaw.

Mercy picked up the green glass chicken dish, dusted it, and said, "I don't see why we can't have the wake at the funeral home. I mean, that's what they're for, ain't it?" She was upset with the whole idea of the wake being held right inside her house.

"'Cause that's what Mother wants, and you know Mother—she gets what she wants," Reatha said. Mercy wasn't surprised by this matter-of-fact answer. As was the case with the majority of family members, Reatha was more than familiar with Granny's ways. She knew there would be no sense in arguing.

How strange it is. We're cleanin' up the livin' room, where no one's ever been allowed to live, for a wake for someone who might not live. Maybe we shoulda been callin' it the dead room.

Certainly won't be no livin' in this room, not ever. It don't make no sense to me.

But Mercy did as she was told. They tugged and pulled the old dresser from the corner, pushing tables aside to allow room for the focal point: the casket. They discussed the most appropriate, stable section in the room for the dreaded casket's placement.

"Probably up against that far wall, over yonder," Reatha said. Then she added, "It'd be safer there."

How many people will come? I don't know; lots from Back Valley, I reckon.

By late afternoon, the frigid outside temperature had crept into the already chilly living room; very little heat came in from the sitting room. There was no fire in the fireplace, of course; it was against Granny's rules. But they would do it anyway. They needed to keep warm while they worked. They both giggled aloud at the thought of doing something that might get them in trouble with Granny. Aunt Reatha scurried to build the forbidden fire.

Lordy, Granny'll have one o' her conniption fits!

Mercy gathered coal and wood, stacked it carefully, and lit the fire. Immediately, the room began to glow from the warmth of the blaze. Mercy had never before felt warmth and coziness in the living room. Its walls seemed to breathe and come alive for the very first time. After scrubbing, mopping, and straightening the room, they looked with pride on what they had accomplished. By the end of late evening, the room had been transformed.

The linoleum floor is jist a-shinin'. Why, look at Aunt Reatha, walkin' 'round in her new white socks—and she don't even get 'em dirty. What a sight to see! No coal dust on your feet.

Once the two had completed their work, they became concerned about Granny's reaction to the changes they had made. When they heard Uncle Paul's car pull into the front lot, the giggling halted. Mercy and her aunt waited anxiously as Granny crossed the yard, stepped onto the wooden front porch, and opened the front door. The horrified expression on her face said it all.

No, she don't like it. Not in the least, not a bit! She don't understand, don't care about the reason for all our hard work, and don't wanna see any of her old furniture rearranged. She certainly don't want a fire in that fireplace!

"Put out that fire! *Now!*" Granny sputtered. "And put all that furniture back where ye got it!" Stomping out of the living room, she shot Reatha and Mercy a do-as-I-say glare.

Aunt Reatha tried to explain, but Granny would have no part of it. So, they moved the furniture one more time, and doused the flames in the fireplace. They would laugh about it later—but not while Granny was around, of course. Grandpaw didn't pass away at that time, and no one was the worse for the temporary changes in Granny's living room. But from that point on, it became the dead room to Mercy.

Excerpt From "Heart's Ease"
Ella Wheeler Wilcox

And give me something to think about
Something besides my pain;
And let me labor throughout the day
With a busy hand and brain.
From the flush of morn 'til the gloom of night
With never a time to weep;
And then in the gloaming let me turn
Like a weary child to sleep.

CHAPTER 24

OUTSMARTIN' GRANNY

Mercy's aunts and uncles were always unfailingly kind to her when they visited. They brought drinks and sweets for the family; because of her father's name, Mercy was always partial to R.C. Cola, of course. As usual, the soft drinks and snacks were taken away by Granny and hidden in the closet for safekeeping, seldom to be seen again. In addition to their offerings of kindness, the aunts and uncles sometimes gave Mercy small amounts of money. Mercy did not understand why they were so generous, but she supposed it was because they felt sorry for her, and it was their way of helping Granny cope with the responsibilities of raising grandchildren. Uncle Lawrence was especially generous and thoughtful. At the end of every visit, he would find an excuse to coax Mercy outside on the front porch and then hand her money.

Each time, the same words, "Don't tell yer granny I gave you this," he would say, as he handed her 50 cents or $1, all the while making sure Granny was out of earshot.

"And remember, don't forget your two weeks with Lane in Narrows."

"Oh, thank ye so much!" said Mercy, a big grin on her face.

She was thankful for the extra change to purchase a snack at school or a piece of candy at the grocery store in Cleveland. This time, he had given her a whole dollar—four quarters. But she knew *why*. Mercy was used to this ritual. They played the same game each visit, always for Granny's benefit. She watched Uncle Lawrence start the old 1952 Rambler and listened to its engine grind as he shifted into second gear. He maneuvered out of the lot, through the open gate, and onto the dirt road. Mercy waved to him until she could no longer see the top of the old jalopy. He was such a good uncle, she thought, and she felt a sense of sorrow at watching him leave.

As usual, the end of the ritual came immediately after Uncle Lawrence was out of sight. Mercy expected it every single time. Soon afterward, Granny opened the door, stepped onto the porch and said, "How much money'd he give ye this time?"

"None," Mercy responded, hoping the quarters didn't jingle in her pockets, giving her away.

"Don't lie to me! I know he gave you some. Now, where is it?" Granny yelled.

"He didn't give me much this time, jist 50 cents," Mercy lied.

Reaching out her hand to snatch the coins, Granny said, "Well, give it to me!"

Mercy placed the two quarters into Granny's outstretched hand and sullenly walked away, still hoping the other two quarters didn't jingle and reveal the truth. She planned to use the other 50 cents for her own personal use, just the way Uncle Lawrence had planned it. They both had learned over the years not to reveal the exact amount. Granny always demanded the money, and so they had learned to beat Granny at her own game. Smugly, Mercy walked away, happy that she and Uncle Lawrence had once again outsmarted Granny.

In the beginning, when Mercy was younger, Granny had taken *all* her money. She had been angry and cried because she was confused about why she was not allowed to keep the small change, since her relatives gave it to her. Later, she had refused to take it when it was offered, explaining to her aunts and uncles that Granny would always take the money from her. In the end, they all insisted that she accept their offerings, and the plan to deceive Granny was born.

Always use change, that way Granny can't get all my money. I'll jist buy two ice creams at school with them two quarters. I know Uncle Lawrence don't never give money to Darrell or Gary Wayne. Why's he do that, anyhow? I reckon he sees how Granny favors Darrell and how Grandpaw favors Gary Wayne. Maybe it's his way of evenin' the odds.

Mercy—the entire family, really—had learned not to disagree with Granny. Not ever, not about anything. They could never win. Mercy just learned to outsmart her, not delving into her granny's eccentric behaviors. But she did question other things around her, always seeking answers to why she was so unhappy, why she felt she was such a bad child, why she could not be loved, and why things could not be changed.

The answers never came. One day, someday, Mercy hoped to be able to unravel the mysteries.

Mercy's homeplace in Back Valley

Nell in front of her trailer on Sandy Ridge

Pat and Mercy (potential adoptive parent)

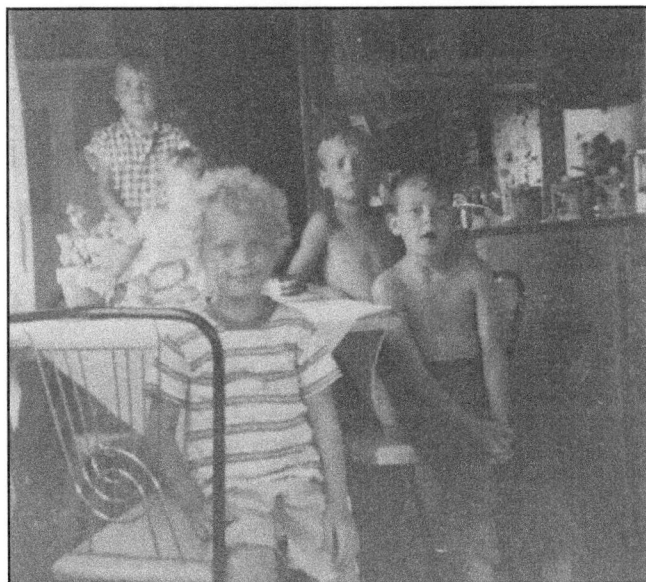

Joyce, Darrell, Gary Wayne, Mercy and Lynn

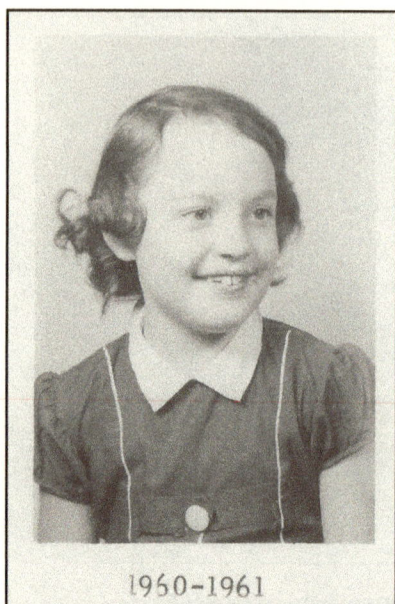

**Young Mercy
in Ohio**

1950-1961

Young R.C.

Cleveland Elementary (4th grade)

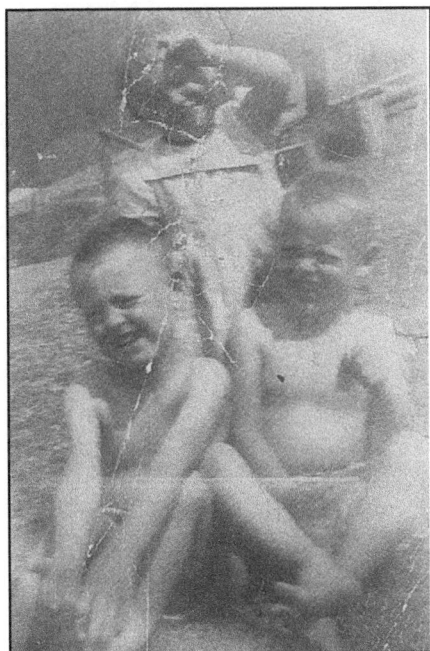

Mercy,
Darrell,
and Gary
Wayne

Mattie and
Daff Musick

Cave in Back Valley

Mattie and Daff Musick in Back Valley

Granny and Nell

CHAPTER 25

VACATION IN NARROWS

The school year ended with Mercy receiving Mrs. Porterfield's Reading the Most Books for the Year Award. Standing proudly in front of the classroom, she accepted the gold necklace with the tiny pendant from her teacher.

Completing homework and getting time for her reading had become harder, with the increased chores and Granny's early bedtime rule. Knowing how much time was involved in school assignments, Mercy had begged to keep the kitchen light on for reading.

But Grandpaw would yell, "I ain't payin' no big juice bill. Turn out them kitchen lights!"

And Mercy would.

On those nights, she had finished the homework and leisure reading with the dim glow from the fireplace. Getting as close as she could to the hearth and sitting on the straight-back cane chair, she had appreciated the tiny patch of light. With stubbornness and tenacity, she had won that reading award, once again proving the payoff of what some deemed as hard work. For Mercy though, it wasn't hard work, just another excuse to do extra reading at home.

With school finished, Mercy was thankful for her uncle's promise of a summer vacation in Narrows. She could not wait to visit with her cousin Elaine, but she also looked forward to spending time with her cousins Linda, Paula, and Ronnie. Her granny had finally agreed to allow her this rare opportunity to leave the valley. On pins and needles, she had waited for Uncle Lawrence's visit. The day had finally arrived. Packed and eager to leave for her vacation, she scrambled to his car, settled herself comfortably inside the old Rambler, and waited…and waited…then waited some more.

"Uncle Lawrence sure likes to talk," she mumbled.

When her uncle's car finally pulled out of the front lot onto the gravel road, she felt no remorse at leaving. As usual, the old car's engine ground as he shifted into second gear. Mercy waved goodbye to her granny until the car topped over the hill and headed toward Cleveland. Leaving the river road, they turned left over the Clinch River bridge and entered downtown Cleveland.

Musick & Owen's grocery store seemed busy, and a cluster of men folk gathered outside the front steps of Fraley's Hardware. As her uncle rounded the stiff curves on Cleveland Mountain, she thought again about how she had been born in Uncle Taze's truck, right here on this mountain road. Which curve, she wondered? And why would her father not talk to her about the birth? She wanted to know all the details of that event, but he had never answered her questions. "Maybe when you're older," he always said.

Passing through Slab Town and Lebanon, they headed north on Highway 19. Within the hour, she spotted the exit to Richlands and Claypool Hill. She knew Bluefield was ahead (where her mother's mother lived), and she steeled herself for the emotions she knew were inevitable.

Where is my mommy? Is she still somewhere in Bluefield? Why hasn't my mommy made contact durin' these ten years she's been gone?

She watched with keen eyes for all the sights along the way while the car cruised through Bluefield, VA and across the state line into Bluefield, WV.

Maybe my mommy is walkin' on one of these streets this very minute and I'll see her. I could catch a glimpse of her. Maybe, just maybe…my mind still can't pull up a clear picture of what she looks like.

Sadness welled within her, and she turned from the window, closed her eyes and pretended to sleep.

I know I probably wouldn't even recognize my mommy. That old photo in the good room don't show a clear enough image for me to recognize my mommy on the street. It's hopeless. Just tuck these thoughts away for another time.

Mercy sat up straight in the seat and launched into a non-stop dialogue with her uncle, just to get her mind off things. They drove through Princeton, then moved on toward Glyn Lyn. She remembered hearing about Glyn Lyn all her life.

Yeah, I remember now; that's where my Uncle Paul and Uncle Denver worked. What a funny name. Glyn Lyn, Glyn Lyn, Glyn Lyn.

Finally, they reached the New River Bridge, leading to downtown Narrows.

Mercy and Elaine were near the same age and enjoyed one another's company, playing together throughout the years. Her cousin was one of those city girls that Mercy envied so often. Elaine lived in downtown Narrows, an unpretentious town located near the city of Blacksburg, not far from the West Virginia border. Elaine was a precocious young girl, and most folks thought her lucky to inherit her mother's olive skin, raven hair, and dark eyes.

I envy her—jist a lil' jealous of her place in life, her good fortune at havin' parents that doted on her, her luck at havin' her own room. But I love her more 'n anythin'.

Elaine rushed out to greet her, a big, wide smile on her face. They hugged, quickly unloaded the car, and scampered off to Elaine's bedroom.

There they listened to Elvis Presley records, singing and dancing along with the rhythm of the music. By nightfall, Mercy was exhausted, so she and her cousin retired for the night. As she lay down on her side of the bed, tucked in beside Elaine, Mercy looked up and beheld a wondrous sight.

Why, there are tiny, gold, shiny stars up on the ceilin'!

"What in the…" Mercy exclaimed as she leapt out of her side of the bed.

"They're jist little stars. I stuck 'em on the ceilin', and they shine at night when the lights go out," Elaine said, laughing and wondering why her cousin became so excited about such a simple thing.

"What a cool idea!" Mercy said.

How nice it must be, to have your own room and decorate it like you want. To put stars on your ceilin' and have permission from your parents to do it! I'm jealous—again.

Later, Mercy visited Aunt Reatha and joined in all their family activities, and chores. Aunt Reatha was a meticulous housekeeper, as well as the head of the household. Uncle Paul worked away from home, and she was left to care for the three children during his absences. Each child knew his or her responsibilities, and carried them out without much ado. They knew they would be rewarded for good behavior and work well done. Aunt Reatha was always fair when she doled out reprimands, and Mercy felt secure knowing she would be treated just like everyone else in the family. When she and her brothers were younger and Aunt Reatha visited Granny, the six children would often squabble. When time came for adult intervention, Aunt Reatha lined all six kids up on the porch in a row, giving each child a switch or two across the legs.

It didn't bother me none. It was the fair thing to do, since we'd all been in the group squabble. There was no "she did it!" or "he did it!" Everyone got switched. And I 'preciated the fairness of it. I love and respect my Aunt Reatha. No showin' favoritism with her. Darrell got the switch, too.

Mercy, already accustomed to following directions and completing chores, found comfort in structured family rules and expectations. Each morning, she and her cousins completed household chores and scurried off to a new activity. That was one of the rules at Aunt Reatha's house: chores first, then play. They made their beds, swept or vacuumed, and straightened the house before they hurried off for more fun.

Mercy found walking to town one of their most exciting adventures; it was an easy trek, since Aunt Reatha lived within the city limits. Her tidy, comfortable, two-story home perched on a steep hill overlooking Main Street. The backyard steps led directly to the house owned by Mrs. Russell (Uncle Paul's mother), and to the sidewalk leading into the town of Narrows.

Five-year-old Ronnie enjoyed tagging along during their frequent jaunts to town or to the park. Mercy, Linda, and Paula took him to the local department store and persuaded him to try on and model a girl's swimsuit once. What a sweet, compliant little boy; he was a picture of innocence standing outside that dressing room, a big smile on his face while he was wearing that colorful one-piece bathing suit. They all laughed, including Ronnie. It was good, clean fun.

Mercy learned to roller skate that summer. Aunt Reatha and Uncle Paul were skilled skaters, and all the children owned their own personal skates.

I can't remember havin' so much fun in my whole life, skatin' 'round and 'round that rink with all my cousins. Swimmin' in the river and sunbathin' was a dream come true. Ridin' bikes on paved streets and havin' a park near your home was the closest thing to a fairy tale life.

All too quickly her vacation ended, and she readied herself for the return to Granny's house. Mercy had watched the way Uncle Paul and Aunt Reatha lovingly interacted with their three children. When Uncle Paul came home on weekends, they all hugged and kissed him affectionately. With his gentle voice, he often begged, "Please rub my feet, rub my feet," and all of them, including Mercy, rubbed and massaged his feet, sometimes until he fell asleep.

The children were allowed to have snacks after supper. Mercy relished the opportunity to serve herself large bowls of ice cream, practically every night. Any snack she wanted, she could have—as long as she cleaned up afterward. And she was allowed to open the refrigerator anytime.

"I don't care how much you kids eat; just clean up your messin' and gommin' afterward," Aunt Reatha said.

"Oh, we will. We will," Mercy promised.

What a normal family, and what lucky children. Why can't I have a mommy and daddy who love one another like Aunt Reatha and Uncle Paul?

But Mercy knew that would likely never be the case, and she accepted the fact she was where she was supposed to be in life.

CHAPTER 26

DR. MENGELE

The year was 1966. By this time, Mercy was 14 years old. She was keenly aware that her grandparents seldom visited doctors, but she'd suffered excruciating toothaches throughout the summer and into the fall. It was time to visit a dentist. Although she had no idea about what to expect, Mercy felt she had no other choice.

An elderly dentist, Dr. Watson, still practiced in downtown Lebanon.

I've heard 'bout that old dentist all my life. Why's he still practicin'? Ain't he too old to still be pullin' teeth? Well, I don't trust him...even one lil' bit.

Once again, she traveled to Lebanon in Uncle Lawrence's old Rambler. Mercy was overwhelmed with dread when she and her uncle finally approached the dentist's office. Not fully realizing what to expect, she hesitantly opened the car door, climbed the steep steps to the old Main Street office, and pushed open the door to a dark, unassuming waiting room. A stifling medicinal smell flooded her nostrils and her throat retched.

I reckon I mighta jist made a mistake by comin' here. My teeth'll be all right. I'll jist leave now.

But it was too late. Dr. Watson slid back the vinyl folding door to his tiny office and walked toward them.

"Hello, I'm Dr. Watson. How can I help you?"

Matter-of-fact voice. No other pleasantries.

Mercy stared at the wrinkles outlining Dr. Watson's face, then said, "Aw, I been havin' some problems with my teeth. Lots of toothaches at night, for a pretty good while now."

"Well, come on in and lemme take a look at 'em."

Yes, he's really old: probably too old to work on my teeth. I'll jist leave now.

Before she could react, Uncle Lawrence prodded her to move forward and Dr. Watson led her toward the single reclining chair behind the vinyl folding door.

"Open ye mouth, now. Let's see how bad they are."

And Mercy opened wide, allowing the old dentist to tilt her head, lift her jaw, and probe inside her mouth.

"Why, those teeth are all rotted out and they're abscessed, both of 'em. We can't save them teeth. They need to be pulled right now."

"Right now?! Today?? Can't you jist put an aspirin on it? That's what I always do at home."

"Naw, that won't work. At least, not this time. Now, jist sit still while I do my work…and I mean sit *still*." Then he proceeded to numb both sides of her mouth.

Stretched out on the reclining chair, Mercy was determined not to show any outward signs of pain. In her world, it was customary not to visit doctors, so she had learned to endure most physical pain without complaint. Focusing on the effects from the numbing gel, Mercy tried to relax and reflect upon other times she had dealt with pain and recovered.

Hadn't she survived the time her daddy held her down and cut her ingrown toenails with a razor blade? Afterward, she'd hobbled to school for two weeks on crutches, but she'd healed without doctors, and without medicine. And all those times she'd endured agonizing earaches—while adults blew smoke circles into her ears to ease the pain. Hadn't Granny insisted that Vicks VapoRub was a miracle drug for most things: sore throats, colds, coughs, and sore muscles? In her granny's home, Rosebud Salve had been the cure for cuts, scrapes, burns, diaper rash, insect bites—even hemorrhoids. Other remedies had cured Mercy's ailments in the past: sassafras root tea for colds, ginger for nausea, turpentine mixed with sugar for worms, witch hazel for styes, and vinegar for an upset stomach. She knew Granny used sheep mutton meat "taller" for chapped hands, and onion poultices placed in hot rags for bronchitis. Mercy wished those salves, poultices, and concoctions could help her now.

But it was not meant to be, not on this day. After a short while, the "Angel of Death" returned and began probing in Mercy's mouth again, this time with a strange type of pliers. Mercy's brave spirit faded as the torture vices wrenched the first tooth.

She screamed, "Ahhhhhhhhhh! Lemme up, lemme up!" She leaned forward, hands clutching the sides of the chair.

Dr. Watson was obviously not pleased with his newest patient. The expression on his face changed instantly to irritation. All flushed now, he leaned toward her and pushed her backwards onto the reclining chair. "Aw, it's ok, you'll be all right now, jist calm down," he insisted.

Calm down? I can't calm down, not with somebody rippin' off my head! I know that medicine takes more time than that to numb this pain! He sure don't have much of a bedside manner for a dentist.

"It ain't workin', it ain't workin'!" Mercy screamed.

"Well, we'll give it a lil' more time. You'll be OK," Dr. Watson said in a patronizing manner. Glancing backward at his uncooperative patient with a scowl on his face, he left to busy himself with another patient.

Much to Mercy's dismay, the dentist soon returned, probing and poking. Out came the pliers again and back into her mouth they went. Mercy screamed even louder than before, "AAHHH!" She bolted upward from the seat, this time frantically trying to push past him.

"You sit back down in that chair! You're scarin' all my other patients!" Dr. Watson reached forward, grabbed the sliding door and hooked it shut, hiding her from the quizzical stares of his patients in the waiting room.

I've read about things like this before, in history class. I wonder if this man could be the real Dr. Mengele, the one who escaped Germany after the war, the one they still can't find. He tortured all them poor, innocent Jews. Lordy, the horrible things he did to them people! Maybe he's hidin' out here in Lebanon, right out in plain sight! I sure am sorry I begged to see that old Dr. Mengele. Lord A' mercy, I ain't never gonna see another dentist again for the rest of my life. I'll probably be left with jist one tooth, jist like Grandpaw.

Recognizing the dentist had lost patience with her, Mercy reconciled herself to enduring whatever unbearable pain was necessary. But she doubted she would ever visit a dentist again, as long as she lived.

On that day, Mercy left Dr. Mengele's office—minus two abscessed teeth.

CHAPTER 27

THE WAKE

Mercy's 10th grade year proved to be a turbulent one. By then, her brother Darrell had come home from Dee-troit. He had grown tired of city life, and she suspected he'd yearned for the familiar surroundings of the mountains, too. But she was puzzled as to why her brother Gary Wayne had not returned also. She still missed him.

As always, she immersed herself in school activities and so-cializing with friends. Granny, on the other hand, was busy with taking care of Grandpaw's continued ailments, and eavesdrop-ping on the telephone's party line. It was 1967, and the local tele-phone services had evolved from operator-assisted calls to rotary dial and party lines throughout Back Valley. News spread via neighborhood gossip and private conversations on the ever-popular party line. Granny, eager to stay connected to current news, kept a vigilant guard on the family telephone.

Mercy thought Granny's obsession humorous. On a regular basis, she caught her granny listening to neighbor's conversations for *long* periods of time. If by chance Mercy came into the sitting room unannounced, Granny would hold up her hand halting her from making any further noise. "Shhh! Be still!" she would whisper, all the while listening to the "goings on" of her neighbors. Mercy also enjoyed talking to her friends on the telephone, but Granny was firm about her 10-minute time limit for conversations.

I don't understand Granny's rules about limitin' my phone calls, while she eavesdrops so long. Some rules jist ain't equal. Like the rules for boys. Then the rules for girls. It don't seem right.

Over time, Granny had fewer opportunities for her telephone entertainment as Grandpaw's conditioned worsened. His frailness, incessant coughing, and breathing difficulties consumed her time and energy. At this point, it was necessary for Mercy and Darrel to help Granny carry Grandpaw to and from the bathroom and assist with family chores, while still maintaining good grades at school. It was a busy time for everyone.

Grandpaw died in his sleep on Halloween Day, 1967. The Grim Reaper of Black Lung had taken another victim. Grandpaw's wake would be held at home, and Mercy and Aunt Reatha, once again, prepared the home for the important family event.

Mercy remembered how conflicted she felt that day. She was at school when she was given the news, and her cousin Carl drove her home in his old black pickup truck. A mixture of emotions flooded through her, but no tears fell. She searched her soul for answers but found none.

As was customary in the mountains, relatives and neighbors carried in food and other necessities to bring comfort and aid to the family. People came from miles around, some she had never known before, to pay their last respects to her grandpaw.

That's the way it is in the mountains. Jist another chance for neighbors to visit, only this time with free food—and I like it.

Most of all, Mercy remembered the strawberry-rhubarb pie a cousin had brought that day. Placed on the open table, tucked among the beans, pickles, relishes, corn, and jams, the sparkling red delicacy immediately beckoned to her. Ignoring Granny's scornful glance, she sliced into the pie.

"That's the best tastin' pie I ever had!" she mumbled with her mouth full. Even before finishing the first bite, she was determined to savor every slice her granny would allow her to have.

"Save that fer company!" Granny snapped, just as Mercy cut off another big slice.

"Why? We got plenty more." Mercy said, as she hurried to take a bite of the slice before Granny could make her put it back.

Mercy ignored Granny's scornful looks and remarks but watched carefully as her granny removed the pie from the table.

That's all right. I'll get some later when company comes! I ain't gonna be outdone, not when it comes to food!

And she did. Mercy had waited patiently until Granny offered some pie to visiting relatives. Cutting herself another slice, she ignored Granny's angry stare, raised eyebrows, and harsh frowns.

I'll never forget that sweet, heavenly flavor of that strawberry-rhubarb pie.

For two nights, the house was abuzz with activity. Mercy had never seen so much company. Gail, one of her friends from school, was there, too. Seldom allowed to have company, Mercy was pleased to have someone visit her, even if it happened to be during Grandpaw's wake. She considered Gail one of those rich kids, so she proudly gave her a tour of her home.

"Here's the bathroom, wanna see it?" Mercy wanted her friend to know there was one *inside* the house.

"We don't *always* have to use the outhouse," Mercy lied.

She had scrubbed that bathroom until it was spotless, just so she could show it off.

I know that bathroom's for company only, but it's one of my proudest moments showin' it off to my friend. Besides, everybody knows you're poor if you still use an outhouse. And Lordy, we couldn't hide that dang thing. Ours sets right out beside the main road!

Grandpaw's body stayed in the living room (or dead room) for two whole nights. During that time, Aunt Reatha took pictures of his cold, stiff, lifeless body inside the casket. Mercy was baffled by the drawn-out ritual, and was restless during those nights. It seemed macabre, even somewhat bizarre to have someone inside a casket in the living room while they all slept in the sitting room.

And how could anybody sleep? What's the purpose of a wake? And why'd they call it a wake when the dead person is obviously not? Who started that ritual? It don't make no sense to me.

Sleep, when it finally came, was followed by tossing and turning and fitful, guilt-ridden dreams about Grandpaw and her inability to mourn his loss.

Conditions worsened at home after Grandpaw's death.

CHAPTER 28

GRANNY'S CLOSET

When Granny scheduled a doctor's appointment in Lebanon, Mercy knew her granny and Aunt Reatha would be gone all day. She and her brother Darrell decided it was an opportune time to break into the secret closet. They would have ample time to remove the lock on the closet door and do some plundering. Happy that the day had finally come, Mercy was still hesitant to sneak into Granny's things. She remembered the time they had stolen the brown sugar. This time they would need to be *extra* careful.

"Granny'll be mad as a wet hen!" Mercy said worriedly.

"Aw, she won't find out. Let's just do it!" Darrell urged, ignoring his sister's warnings.

Mercy watched as her brother forced a screwdriver into the holes of the large, square lock. He jiggled, prodded, and poked until the screws loosened. Finally, the heavy lock dropped to the floor with a dull thud, and the closet door squeaked slightly ajar. Too late to turn back now, Mercy thought.

"Now we've done it! Now we've really done it! We're really in trouble this time. Granny's gonna *kill* us! There could be a dead body in there. Ye never know!" Mercy scolded.

Darrell snorted, "Aw, quit whinin'. She ain't gonna find out nothin'! And there ain't no dead body in there!"

I reckon we've gone too far this time. Bein' nosey and plunderin' is gonna git us in real trouble. What will we find in there? All those years of Granny hidin' things in this closet; there's gotta be some reason. She's gonna skin us alive. I jist know it! Maybe Granny does *have a dead body in there. Everybody in the family jokes 'bout that all the time.*

The heavy, solid wood door swung open, and the wonders of the closet revealed themselves for the first time. Mercy stared at rows of shelves filled with quilt pieces. She picked up the tiny pieces of cloth, rubbing her fingers across wool, cotton, and polyester fabrics. But just as quickly, she placed them back neatly onto the stacked piles.

Better make sure everythin' still looks untouched so Granny won't know it's been moved.

Darrell began his search as they both jockeyed for space in front of the closet. Carefully feeling around the shelves, Mercy reached far into the back, past a pile of rags, and found a bag of horehound candy. It was her granny's favorite. She reached into the crumpled brown paper poke, all the way to the bottom, and grabbed a piece.

No tellin' how long this has been in here. That Gawd-awful taste coats the inside of my mouth. I tried it once before; I re-member now. I'll eat about anythin', but not this stuff. I never could understand why Granny loved that horrible taste: bitter, somewhere between root beer and licorice. And what a terrible name—horehound. It sounds kinda nasty, like a bad word. I don't even like sayin' that word, horehound....horehound...horehound. Wonder where that candy got its name, anyhow.

They carefully rummaged past the stacks of newspapers and old photographs, and finally found a true delicacy: a full carton of orange-flavored Nehi pop. Tucked away in back on the floor of the closet, all six bottles were covered with years of accumulated dust and dirt. But what a treat! Darrell reached for his pocketknife, stuck the blade under the metal cap and opened a drink for each of them. Standing outside the closet, they eagerly savored the sweet, delectable flavor of the treasured soda pop.

"Wow, how long ye reckon she's had 'em in there?" Mercy asked after the first gulp, already prepared for the second good-sized swallow.

"Who knows? Let's see what else she's got," Darrell said.

And they searched, certain they would find more treasures.

Now, look at this. There it was, that pair of scissors Granny was famous for hidin'---her favorite pair. And books and magazines, but nothin' excitin'.

There were bags of Christmas candy: boxes of peppermint stick candy, and mixed hard candy, orange, red, green and yellow. Mercy loved those, and she eagerly bit into one before she realized they had hardened and toughened over time.

"Yuk! Them things probably been in here for years!" she said.

I sure hate the thought of any candy goin' to waste, just bein' hoarded right outa my reach all this time inside the closet.

"I'll eat 'em anyway. No sense wastin' nothin'."

As usual, Darrell ignored her. He was too busy poking, pushing, and lifting everything out of the way, looking for anything else of interest.

And here's Grandpaw's favorite, chocolate haystack candy with the vanilla centers. What a real treat! I'll jist eat some of all of it! Serves Granny right for hidin' all this good stuff! Now what else is in here?

She found colorful, tiny hexagonal fabric pieces for Granny's trip-around-the-world-quilt, needles, and spools of colorful thread and bobbins for the old Singer sewing machine. Then she uncovered medicines: Rosebud Salve, Vicks VapoRub, cod liver oil, and turpentine. There were obituary notices and scores of outdated *Lebanon News* and *Bristol-Herald Courier* newspapers.

The hours flew by, and they were exhausted from their search for hidden treasures. Time was running out, and they decided they had searched enough. There wasn't anything worth the risk of being caught. Granny had nothing of any real value, simply a large collection of household junk.

CHAPTER 29

THE STRANGE VISITOR

The 1960s brought revolutionary changes to America, even to Mercy's mountains. Without a doubt, it was a drastic change from the more complacent 1950s. This new era was a time of social unrest: anti-Vietnam Conflict protests, civil rights movements, riots, and equality for women. Boys wore longer hair, bell-bottom pants, and boldly-colored paisley shirts. Girls wore mini-skirts, hot pants, and panties that matched their short dresses. Like most teens, Mercy took note of it all and wanted to be a part of this changing culture.

She had refused to wear the long dresses Grandpaw insisted she wear. He had been critical of her hair, clothes, and makeup, but she had insisted on dressing like the other girls at school. She couldn't imagine wearing dresses down to her ankles like Granny.

I remember Grandpaw fussin' at me. "You're always primpin'!"
But I never paid him no mind. I know these short miniskirts and fish-
net hose are against Granny's Baptist beliefs. Whatever that means;
I ain't sure. Fire and brimstone, hell and damnation for wearin' them
short skirts! Why, Granny probably wants me to wear an apron too,
and maybe even a diaper on my head.

Pushing those thoughts back into her mind, Mercy meticulously combed and wound layers of her shoulder length hair around brush rollers. That afternoon, she was going on a special date and wanted to look her best. She knew she was getting ready early, but it would take time for her hair to dry, and she wanted it to flip just right. Earlier in the day, she had carefully filled the old, round metal tub with rain water from the cistern. By mid-afternoon, the water was tepid to the touch, just right for her to sit in and bathe. She knew she couldn't use the family bathtub; that was against Granny's rules. The bathtub was reserved for company, she remembered. Her skin, still moist from the fresh rainwater and perfumed soap, now felt soft and refreshed. She had refused the use of her granny's lye soap this time; she detested the lingering scent that clung to her body after using it.

Certainly, this was a special night. It was one of her first *real* dates, a double date. Granny was especially strict about her dating anyone, and insisted that her brother Darrell accompany her, with his date. But since he was out of town on this night, Mercy could enjoy a special evening without Darrell's presence. She would double date with her cousin Bobbie.

"Don't ferget! Be back here at eleven!" Granny hollered as Mercy, along with Bobbie and their two dates, pulled away from the front lot and out onto the river road.

Mercy could never forget that 11 o'clock curfew; she didn't want to anger her granny, so she kept an eye on her watch all the way through Honaker, Finney, and Back Valley. She and Bobbie carried on a constant conversation with one another, only occasionally remembering to include their dates. It was an uneventful night. Pleased to have beaten the curfew, Mercy and Bobbie entered the front lot, crossed the yard and stepped onto the front porch precisely at 11:00.

Somethin's out of place; there's a strange car parked in the front lot. Who can it be this late? And why are they here? Probably just one of my relatives come to pay a visit and stay awhile. It ain't all that unusual to have visitors, but I didn't know 'bout 'em comin'. Maybe they even surprised Granny. Well, I'm pleased; I love company. Granny's nicer to me when company's 'round, not as hateful. I look forward to all the company I can have.

As Mercy entered the living room and moved toward the sitting room, she heard an unfamiliar voice.

Somethin' ain't right.

Her scalp prickled and tiny goose bumps stood out on her arms and legs.

That's a woman's voice. Seems familiar somehow. Where've I heard it before?

Mercy walked slowly into the sitting room and saw a strange woman sitting on Granny's feather bed.

Don't that woman have sense enough to know she's breakin' one of Granny's rules?! Don't sit on the bed. Never. *That woman jist don't know Granny's rules. There's somethin' familiar in that woman's smile, and that auburn hair, those eyes. But that smile... Where've I seen it before? And that laugh. That raspy, loud voice.*

Then Mercy knew. She recognized just the slightest resemblance to the faded photo in the good room.

It was her mother, Nell.

"A Girl"
Ezra Pound

The tree has entered my hands,
The sap has ascended my arms,
The tree has grown in my breast-
Downward,
The branches grow out of me, like arms.
Tree you are,
Moss you are,
You are violets with wind above them.
A child—so high—you are,
And all this is folly to the world.

CHAPTER 30

CHRISTMAS AWAY FROM HOME

Mercy hoped the day had finally arrived. Her mother (she was too old to call her mommy now) had returned for her—at last. Now she would have the mother she had always dreamed about through the years: a mother to love her, cuddle her, and wipe away the endless tears she'd shed. A *real* mother. Not a stepwitch like the one in Michigan, but a *real* one.

"Mother?" Mercy whispered softly. "Is that you?" And she walked hesitantly to the bedside to greet her. Mercy's mind numbered the times she had needed her over the past 10 years.

Where has she been? And why didn't she come for me sooner?

Nell said, "It's me." Nothing more, nothing less. And then she smiled.

Mercy noted it was the same smile as in the faded photograph in the good room, and the same auburn-colored hair. Sadly, she felt the lack of emotion in her mother's response; just that hoarse, raspy voice identified to Mercy that she was truly who she said she was.

Nell rose from the feather bed. Mother and daughter awkwardly hugged, and just as quickly stepped away from one another. It was not the meeting Mercy had expected. But it was a start.

Glancing across the room at her granny, Mercy said, "Mother, why're you here?"

She'd already seen the scorn on her granny's face, and knew the answer to her own question.

I reckon I know without even askin'. Granny called for my mother to come and take me away.

The threats to send her to the home in Grundy had long since ended; her father, although still in Michigan, had insisted Mercy not be sent to an orphanage for unwanted children.

Granny's done this before. No matter how hard I try, Granny is always wantin' to get rid of me. Granny will never accept me, or love me. And now I'm faced with another move. I jist know it. I reckon I'll be livin' with my mother now in Bluefield.

"To take you with me. Your granny called," Nell said. Matter-of-fact, no detailed explanation

I was right. It isn't the answer I wanted to hear, but it's what I expected. Not "I've missed you and wanted to see you," but "Just come with me." She came because she felt there was no other choice.

Later, Mercy couldn't recall a large part of their awkward conversation. A dark cloud hovered over her as she packed her clothes and left with her mother for Bluefield.

Another home, another school. Oh, how I'm gonna miss Barbara Ann, Linda Joann, and Gail, and all my other friends. Even my teachers. How will they know where I am? I can't call 'em, it's way too late at night. This visit from my mother is a complete surprise. There's no time: not even to call my daddy. And how will Daddy feel about this? I'm sure he don't know.

And so, Mercy left Back Valley, once again with the belief she would never return to her beloved home. She left late in the night, in the middle of winter, during Christmas break, going to live in a new home in Bluefield, WV.

As she passed over the threshold at the front door, Mercy glanced backward at her granny. She saw no regret, no sadness in her granny's face at seeing her leave. Just relief, she suspected. As she walked through the front lot beside her mother, the piercing winter wind howled at her back, pushing her forward just as western winds cast tumbleweeds across a prairie.

She'd spend Christmas for the first time in her memory with her mother, Joyce, and baby Randy. Once she got to her new home, she had an awkward reunion. Mercy was seeing her sister Joyce for the first time since they were small children. Mercy was surprised by what she saw. Joyce was now a tiny, thin figure. Her long, white hair framed her haggard face. Mercy was startled by how different she and her sister appeared. There was no real family resemblance, but Joyce did look somewhat like her brother Gary Wayne. Nor did baby Randy look like Mercy. His thick, auburn hair curled on top of his head and over its sides.

Looks like he needs a haircut. And he ain't a baby anymore.

His big smile immediately tugged at her heart, and she was charmed by his vibrant, boyish 10-year-old personality.

Then two smaller, much younger boys scampered through the door.

Who are they? And where'd they come from? I heard stories that my mother ran away from my daddy with another man. Are those two little boys his children? And hers? How could she! You mean, my mother abandoned her children, and then had two more babies?!

Her emotions, rampant now, turned to rage, hate, and then self-pity as she was introduced to Terry and Michael, the two little boys who had replaced Mercy, Gary Wayne, Darrell, and Lynn.

Another question. Why did mother take Joyce and Randy with her? Doesn't she love all of us the same?

Mercy scolded herself, since she already knew the answer to that question. It wasn't possible for parents or grandparents to love all children the same. She had witnessed that time and again throughout the years. She must stop expecting too much from life.

Eventually, Mercy was introduced to her stepfather, Ray. Shocked, she stood motionless and simply stared at his pocked, acne-riddled face and the pronounced scarring of his features

Lowering her head, she said, "Hello" before realizing he had already reached to embrace her. He was a stout man, and Mercy was instantly uncomfortable with his touch. He's trying too hard to get me to like him, she thought. But she dismissed her feelings about this new, strange, unattractive man who had replaced her daddy in her mother's life.

Mercy wasn't pleased with her new home in downtown Bluefield. The small 1920s house and yard mimicked the architecture of the other homes on the street. Much like a coal camp or mill camp, these houses were constructed nearly touching each other, with little space to play and no room to run in the woods, build a tree house, or swing on grapevines. Furnished with mismatched antiques and old photographs haphazardly hanging on walls, the inside lacked both warmth and appeal. Because the house was already bursting at its seams with four children and three adults, Mercy was certain her visit would be a short one—not a permanent move. She was confused as to how this gloomy, overstuffed house could hold even one more person. Secretly, she hoped it couldn't.

The following day, Mercy and her sister Joyce begged to go window shopping. Since it was the Christmas holiday, her mother allowed them this rare trip. Both girls lunged across the front porch, skipped down the front sidewalk, and ran down the steep steps onto the side street. Leading straight to downtown Bluefield, the sidewalks would allow Mercy and Joyce to shop without fear of getting lost.

After all, I reckon I survived livin' outside Detroit, I can survive Bluefield.

They pranced around town, poking and prodding into each sale aisle, hoping their small amount of shopping money would allow for at least one purchase. At long last, Mercy sweet-talked her sister into buying a fashionable mini-dress. After wandering in and out of more clothing stores, they both giggled about their purchase, a dress with red, yellow, and blue horizontal stripes, which was meant to flatter Joyce's wiry figure.

Mercy enjoyed every moment she spent with Joyce and Randy. She couldn't have been happier to watch Randy roll his little cars and imitate race sounds around and around the rugs on the hardwood floors. And to watch Joyce look through beans for rocks, then wash them, and boil the pinto beans in the tiny, outdated kitchen. Mercy was impressed with Joyce's independence and ability to cook. She had never been allowed to do that at her granny's house.

Two days later, on Christmas Eve, Mercy dreamed about the gift she would receive from her mother. She surveyed the small cedar tree in the corner of the already cramped living room. It seemed to disappear behind the purple garland, shiny glass balls, and silver icicles. Not much better than the little tree we used to have in Back Valley, she thought.

After a while, Mercy couldn't stop herself. She simply had to look for her gift in the pile of wrapped boxes beneath the tree. As she searched, peeking at each name tag, it seemed there was not one package with her name on it. Surely this isn't so, she thought. Although her mother hadn't planned for her to be here this year, Mercy felt certain she would have a gift, even if bought at the last moment.

Maybe it's been hidden: a special surprise just for me, to be brought out later since I'm a special guest this year. A gift to be opened in front of everyone, even the other boys, just to show everyone how special I am.

Christmas morning arrived, much to the excitement of all the children. But Mercy was especially eager to receive that special gift that would certainly be given to her in some exceptional manner. She patiently watched while the other children ripped and tore into their presents, all the while wondering when hers would come.

A new mini-dress? New jewelry? Maybe a pair of fishnet hose that I'll just love. Makeup or a new purse? A new pair of loafers would be perfect!

Mercy had never really believed in Santa Claus. She had always known the truth, somehow. But she would go along with this bit of Christmas lore, for the sake of Randy and the smaller boys. She remembered other Christmas mornings with Granny and Grandpaw and her brothers, Darrell and Gary Wayne. Each year, placed in front of the fireplace was a half-filled brown paper bag for each of them. Inside were assorted candies and one orange. One Christmas, Aunt Reatha had brought her a lavender raincoat and a pink plastic purse. That beautiful purse had become Mercy's favorite gift that year. For two weeks, she never let it leave her sight. Taking that purse with her on the first day back to school from Christmas break became an obsession for her; she wanted to show it off to everyone. That morning, she had placed her prized purse in the living room while waiting on her bus to arrive—and it froze and burst in the arctic cold of that living room. Years later, she could still recall the shape, color and special aura of that favorite Christmas present, and her sorrow at its loss.

Another year, she had received a beautiful bride doll which Granny tucked away in the good room. She refused to allow Mercy to play with it at all.

"Jist look at it. It's too purty to play with," Granny said.

By now, the last of the presents were being ripped apart by the boys. Mercy held her breath as she watched the unwrapping of one final present.

Now, it's my turn. What?! I just can't believe I didn't get a gift. There's nothin' for me. Absolutely nothin'! Not one single pitiful lil' gift.

Noticing the stricken look on Mercy's face, Ray attempted an explanation. "We're sorry we didn't get you anything, Mercy. We just didn't have time, and we didn't even know you were gonna be here, remember?"

"Oh, that's OK. It was fun just watching y'all open yours." Mercy lied, forcing a smile while watching the boys romp and play with their new toy trucks.

They won't never see me cry! Never. Not never. I hate 'em, hate 'em all. 'Specially them boys. I ain't never been special to nobody!

Mercy licked her wounds throughout the night, and the next day she told her mother she wanted to return to Back Valley. She knew Granny probably didn't want her, but she felt there was no place for her in her mother's home. She noticed that her mother didn't beg or insist she stay.

On the telephone, Mercy begged, "Granny, please let me come home. I'll do anythin', anythin' you want. Just please let me come back home." She begged and begged some more. And cried.

"Well, I reckon, but only if ye'll mind me and won't be sassy!" Granny said.

And Mercy promised. And promised again.

Even though I ain't never understood what it is I done that made Granny so mad, I'll promise anythin'.

She quickly packed her bags once again for the return trip to Back Valley, back to what was familiar and comfortable to her. Back to the only place she really loved, her mountains, with her group of friends, and her blood kin. Mercy sensed her mother was pleased with her decision to leave, since she had not begged Mercy to stay.

She had lived two weeks with her mother. Long enough to realize there was no room for another child in her mother's life. Mercy must give up any hope that she would ever have a mother-daughter relationship. She left with unanswered questions, ones she didn't dare ask her mother.

Why did my mother never visit me? And how does a mother abandon her children? Why, even old stray cats drag their tiny kittens to safety. They lick, clean, and feed 'em, no matter how many in the litter. Even when Grandpaw rounded 'em up, placed 'em in a sack and drowned 'em in the Buckeye Hole, the mothers meowed and mourned the loss of their babies. How can my mother not care?!

And so, Mercy returned to Back Valley, the only place she had ever found consolation, carrying with her all the unanswered questions.

CHAPTER 31

PLAY PURTIES

On the porch, Mercy stood looking at the winter's sun rising in the east. Rays of early morning sunlight crept across the field toward the bottomland, erasing the last hint of darkness and slowly lighting the shrouded barn, locust trees, and surrounding hillside as they inched toward the home place. Still as a bronze statue, she stood silently, waiting for the sunshine to reach her. As it edged its way across her feet, she lifted her eyes and allowed the light to gently caress her face. She smiled and welcomed the New Year. She was home again.

Reveling in the warmth of the early morning rays, Mercy gazed across the familiar fields. She thought about her recent visit with her mother. She missed her sister, but not her mother. It was strange that she had waited all those years to view her mother's face, but now couldn't mourn for her dream: the loving mother she'd always wanted, but knew she'd never have. She felt Joyce was so fragile and needed her; she couldn't dismiss the feeling that she had abandoned her sister.

What was wrong? What was my sister hidin'? I must try hard to forget her. Nothin' can be done. No sense cryin' over spilled milk. I'll probably never see Joyce or baby Randy ever again.

Still entrenched in her own thoughts, Mercy's legs propelled her toward the open field. She'd crossed the foot log across the creek without even realizing it. Through misty eyes, she reminded herself that she was lucky. She had a roof over her head, plenty to eat, and lots of friends.

Mercy smiled as she recalled the time her brothers Darrell and Gary Wayne had built an old wagon on this spot.

The one with the scrap board sides and rusty bottom. They pulled Lynn 'round and 'round the narrow path surroundin' the tobacco field. Right out beside the old garden, past the raspberry patch and the foot log leadin' to the hog lot, and wrecked her. Jist dumped her right out on the tobacco field. Lynn had laughed and laughed! What a big smile and loud cackle she had that day.

Later, Mercy and her sister had returned to the front porch to enjoy a whole box of Vanilla Wafers, a treat Lynn had brought along with her, since she knew Granny would not have sweets to offer during her visit.

It would've been nice, havin' another girl 'round to share dolls and my miniature tea set. But I've outgrown 'em now: don't play with toys anymore. I boxed 'em away and stored 'em under my bed. My favorite teddy bear, tucked away and protected from strangers. Wonder if the toys are still where I put 'em?

Nostalgic at the thoughts of her toys, she decided it was time to rummage through the cardboard box and relive precious childhood memories. Loping back across the open field, Mercy carefully crossed the foot log over the branch and stepped into the front lot. She followed the well-worn path into the yard, and took the front steps with one giant stride right onto the wooden porch. Mercy was eager to reunite with her childhood toys.

They always make me feel better.

She flitted past the living room and into the sitting room. Carefully lifting the edge of the yellow chenille coverlet, she peeked under the bed. There was nothing there except the last remnants of dust balls her granny had missed while cleaning earlier. Nothing!

Where is my special box, the one I carefully packed away and loaded up with my childhood play purties?

Her heart skittered in her chest and a sense of panic gripped her as she continued her search throughout the house. Ransacking the entire home, even the good room, she couldn't find them. And then she knew. Granny had gotten rid of them while she'd been gone. At that instant, Granny stepped into the good room demanding, "Why're ye in here?!"

"Where's my old box o' toys?" Mercy asked.

"I gave 'em away." Granny answered without batting an eye.

Trying to hold back her anger, Mercy blurted, "You gave 'em away?"

"Aw, you're too big for 'em now. You don't need 'em. I give 'em to the lil' neighbor girls down the road. Now, get outa the good room!" Granny said.

"But you gave 'em away without even askin' me first! I wanted 'em, wanted to keep 'em forever!" Mercy sassed.

"Aw, you didn't need all that junk!"

"Well, I'm gonna get 'em back!" Mercy shouted.

She quickly left the good room and sprinted through the screen door back onto the front porch. Despite her granny's warnings, she was determined to locate her cherished toys.

How could she! My favorite teddy bear! Oh, how he must miss me! Well, I'll jist go right into that *house and demand 'em back! Granny has definitely overstepped her boundaries this time. I'm so mad I could spit!*

Mercy knew it wouldn't be easy. Earlier memories of *that* house angered her when she remembered how she had been humiliated there. She stepped onto the graveled road leading to *that* house, and she knew there was no going back on her calculated plan. Although she had promised Granny not to be sassy, her frustration kept her from being rational.

I'll jist stomp right in there and take 'em! Ain't' no stoppin' me!

Racing to the river road, she dashed past the Rocky Fork spring. There would be no time to sample the fresh spring water this trip; but Mercy paused briefly and stared at the old cave that jutted outward beside the main road. She and her brothers had played inside that cave as children, ignoring the warnings of their granny. It had been a scary experience, but since she was older now, the opening in the cliff seemed less ominous, less challenging. She was still awed by its presence, though. Her earlier adventures inside the cave had been reckless, and she was relieved they had survived those experiences. She needed to hurry; she didn't want to pass the open cave after sundown.

As she moved forward, Mercy hesitantly glanced backward at the cave, a cautionary act just to make certain she wasn't being followed.

As she continued the short trek down the dirt road, her thoughts regressed again to earlier years. She had spent hours researching and completing a science project with specimens discovered on the North Hill and the river road. The leaf book had been an easy task; she had collected most of her specimens from this very site. Jack-in-the-pulpit, sassafras, Lombardy poplar, chestnut, and mountain laurel were abundant throughout Back Valley, especially here.

From the corner of her eye, a slight movement caught Mercy's attention. Glancing backward in the direction of the cave, she hesitated and cautiously scanned her surroundings. In the past, the sounds from the forest, particularly in this section of road, had unnerved her. Swaying in the winter's breeze, oak and hickory trees appeared to reach outward and gesture as she passed, their winter-bare branches like tentacles on a giant octopus.

Her body trembled. The winter's chill and her imagination caused her body to stiffen. In her flurry, Mercy had forgotten her winter coat.

Since she was a child, Mercy had lugged buttermilk from *that* house right past the old cave, sometimes near nightfall. It was a chore she had loathed. Filled to the brim, the old gallon jars, capped with wax paper and sealed with lids, were cumbersome for a small child. But she had managed. She remembered grasping the jugs, closing her eyes and sprinting past the cave.

Slosh...slosh...slosh. *That nasty buttermilk had always oozed through the wax paper. Right out on my clothes. Never did like buttermilk. Still don't like it! I'm sure glad I ain't carryin' them jugs today. Time to get movin'. I reckon I'll never be able to get over the heebie-jeebies of walkin' by this cave. Yes, that's all it is: jist the wind. My mind always plays tricks on me.*

Mercy's feet flew like the wind. This time, she didn't glance backward.

She needed to prepare herself for the confrontation that would surely take place. Like a cog in a machine, her mind raced to keep pace with her feet. Flashes of angry scenarios played out in her head; she struggled to alter each scene for a more favorable outcome, but she couldn't get them to end well.

As she neared the main gate to *that* house, she felt the tiny hairs on her skin spiking upward.

Jist like a dog sensin' danger.

Inhaling a deep breath, Mercy stepped inside the yard, prepared for battle but without a solid plan of action.

How can I get them toys without makin' a big fuss? Granny'll have a hissy fit if I'm sassy. How can I simply ask for my toys back without makin' that woman mad? And probably seein' them two lil' girls cry?

As she neared the steps to the back door, Mercy saw the pair of seven-year-old girls scampering past their mother into the side yard. With a lump filling her throat, she stared as one of the girls clutched her favorite toy. It was Teddy! With a new owner. Mixed feelings of anger, mourning, and fear filled her.

Sorrow gripped Mercy's heart; she glared while Teddy was tossed in the air, dragged through the dirt, and thrown on the woodpile in the far corner of the yard. Trying to conceal her real feelings, Mercy lowered her face and pretended not to see Teddy. She made a simple attempt to hide the tears that had welled up and threatened to overflow at any moment. Throughout the years, Mercy had learned the futility of crying.

And they won't see me cry on this day, neither. I refuse to shed even one single tear. 'Specially in front of that woman. Why, I jist wanna run and grab Teddy right off o' that woodpile and run right home again.

Forcing herself to move forward, Mercy focused on finding out the fate of her other toys. *That* woman stood by the kitchen door, a questioning expression already firmly planted on her face.

"Hi, y'all." Mercy said

"What's ye doin' today?" said *that* woman.

"Aw, jist thought I'd come to see the lil' uns," she lied. And she glanced again in the girls' direction. She added, "Boy, those girls sure have grown."

"Yeah, they're big girls now. Seems like they growed since yesterday."

Mercy knew this was a critical moment.

That *woman don't fool me none. Granny's probably already called her on the gossip line. That blasted telephone! I mustn't be disrespectful. I mustn't be sassy, or Granny'll send me away to that home in Grundy, that home for girls. Like she's always threatenin' to do, time and time again.*

"How're they enjoyin' my old toys?"

"Ah, they like 'em, 'specially that lil' tea set. I seen 'em just yesterday, wilin' away the day just sippin' from them lil' cups and saucers."

Mercy's heart sank. An uncomfortable lump tightened deep in her throat. She couldn't swallow and breathing became harder. She was acutely aware of the awkwardness of the situation but stood still, waiting for *that* woman to take action, to say something else—anything else.

But *that* woman simply stood in the same warped position as before: scrawny legs and knees bent backwards in an awkward position that bowed her entire body. Her stance caused her lower stomach and chest to protrude forward. Her face, like that of many older women, was creased with deep lines. Long strands of hair, some dark and some gray, were pulled away from her face with a rubber band. The youthful shine to her face and hair had long since disappeared. Lye soap and regular use of rubber bands had damaged her face and hair.

Mercy realized the attempt to recover her beloved toys was a failure. The anger inside her had eased enough for her to be more rational, and think through her actions. She would not, could not, do anything.

She said, "Well, I'll be gettin' back now. Got to get home before dark."

"Well, tell your granny I'll send more buttermilk when I can."

As Mercy sauntered through the backyard gate, she caught one final glimpse of Teddy. She couldn't bear the thought of her special friend abandoned to suffer the fate of the piercing cold, the possibility of future downpouring rains, or even the snow that was predicted to fall throughout this night.

She yearned to caress him one last time, but she knew there was no use. Unable to contain her tears any longer, she picked up her pace and sprinted toward the main road.

The tears flowed freely then.

Mercy mumbled, "Teddy, oh Teddy, I'll never forget you. No matter where I go, no matter how old I get, you'll always be in my heart. Thank you for bein' my friend for so many years. Just remember, I didn't *give* you away…like I was given away. You were taken *from* me! Forgive me for not fightin' harder for you. Goodbye, Teddy. I loved you," And she sobbed…and sobbed… and sobbed some more.

Teddy, the inanimate object who had listened to her innermost secrets, her hopes and dreams for the future. And allowed her to shed her tears on his brown, furry body, without complaint or scolding her for crying. Unconditional love, something she could not yet fully define.

Retracing her steps up the river road, Mercy slowed her pace and allowed herself to mourn the loss of her childhood friend.

And her childhood.

I must get all the cryin' done before goin' home. I made the right choice. Granny would've sent me away to another home. And maybe this time it would've been for good. I don't think I could bear that. Not again. Never again.

Crisp gusts of winter air began to blow through the natural tunnel and gap in the mountains. Advancing from her rear, the wind propelled her forward, toward home. Mercy's long chestnut hair flew about her face, shrouding her ears and cheeks. She was unable to turn around, even for a brief glance backwards at the cave. The wind shrieked. *Keep moving...keep moving...keep moving.*

She did. And she never looked back.

CHAPTER 32

I-N-G

An affluent, well-bred millionaire gazing at poverty from an upscale Manhattan flat cannot relate to homelessness. In the same way in Mercy's world, her kinfolk couldn't relate to the unnecessary use of proper English. Emphasis on farm work, pride in maintaining inherited family land, and rearing God-fearing children were more important. Mercy knew her kinfolk placed little value on irrelevant, material possessions and "uppity talk." Marrying a Yankee was discouraged; time and again, she'd overheard her granny say, "Why'd they wanna go and marry a Yankee for?" Neighbors gossiped about strangers moving into the area, and were suspicious of Northern habits. Having lived in Detroit, Mercy questioned the Yankees' ideology and their long-standing habit of making fun of mountain speech. At every opportunity,

Mercy mocked *their* speech.

During her one-year stint in Michigan, Mercy suspected she had learned why Yankees added I-N-Gs at the end of verbs.

I reckon they jist wanna be uppity! No other reason makes sense to me.

But Mercy didn't understand the significance of proper English, not until Mrs. Reid. She could recall the exact day. She envisioned it as if it had happened yesterday; her thoughts instantly propelled her to the event.

"Okay. Now class, today's lecture will be chiefly related to the usage of verbs…and how we must learn to pronounce the I-N-G at the end of them. Do you understand, class?"

Lifting her hand into the air, Mercy was the first to question what she knew must be on everyone else's mind. She said, "Whaddaya mean? I don't understand."

In her most precisely articulated voice, Mrs. Reid said, "Well, what I'm referring to is how my students often overlook full articulation of verbs in their sentences." Then she paused to gaze across the classroom, an effort to monitor reaction and understanding from her students.

Mercy waited, as did everyone else in the class. Her admiration of Mrs. Reid was indisputable. She relished this teacher's lectures and her skill in bringing characters to life. In her polished manner, Mrs. Reid could compare and contrast characters in a novel, connecting them to current events and the time and place represented in the novel. Through those shared elements, she was able to help her students more clearly understand complex literature.

But what in the world is this teacher talkin' 'bout?

Mrs. Reid had recently moved from Richmond to the nearby town of Lebanon. Like most others, Mercy viewed Mrs. Reid as a foreign transplant—maybe even a Yankee—but she welcomed this new teacher's fresh, worldly views. Mercy enjoyed the challenge in the classroom, and Mrs. Reid encouraged Mercy's love of reading. A staunch, no-nonsense teacher, Mrs. Reid enjoyed lecturing. This was the type of day it was in her classroom.

Uh-oh, here comes the lecture part.

As if a hypnotist had verbalized a command, Mercy slouched forward in her seat, placed her right hand under her chin, planted her elbow on the desk, and gazed across the room at her teacher. She looked deeply into Mrs. Reid's face, counted the wrinkle lines on her forehead, noted the faint tint of her makeup, and silently traced the lines surrounding her mouth as if observing her for the first time. Daydreaming.

What is it about her that seems so mysterious to me? She's plain: jist a plain-oh-jane teacher, probably beautiful in her younger days. She always stands up so straight, even when she walks. But somethin' about her makes me wanna learn. I can't decide if it's the salt-and-pepper hair that makes me think she's been teachin' for centuries, or the way she tilts her head while frownin', which forces me to pay attention. Makes me wanna listen.

"Mercy, pay attention. Tell me what I just said."

Mercy jerked up, raising her body to a more erect position in her desk, and refocusing her eye contact with Mrs. Reid. Mercy coughed, perhaps even a bit showy, and then uttered, "Aw, you were talkin' about us not addin' I-N-G to our verbs, right?"

Like the tempo of an Indian chant, Mrs. Reid didn't skip a beat. She responded, "That's partially correct, but repeat what you just said, Mercy."

Oh, boy, I'm on the bad side of the teacher now! What'd I do? Is this somethin' like writin' I will pay attention in class five hundred times, except you jist say it out loud, over and over, five hundred times?

"You mean *exactly* what I jist said?"

"Yes, the same thing."

Certain she was being ridiculed for not paying attention, Mercy said, "Word for word?"

I love daydreamin', gettin' lost in my own thoughts.

"Yes. The same thing, just repeat it."

"Well, I said you were talkin' to us about not addin' I-N-G to our verbs."

Gliding expertly across the room, Mrs. Reid positioned her body directly in front of Mercy. Uncomfortable with the encroachment on her personal space, Mercy's small frame leaned backward into the seat, as if her body could somehow become a piece of her chair. The middle of her spine inched backward, attempting to fill in the tiny air spaces between her body and the curved wood frame. Becoming one and the same.

What's that woman want from me, anyhow?

Mrs. Reid prodded, "Yes, that's correct. Now, Mercy, state the verbs in your sentence."

Phew! Is that all she wanted?! That ain't no problem. But I'm about verbed out from conjugatin' all them French verbs in my French class.

"*Said* is a verb, *talkin'* and *addin'* are verbs, and…oh yeah, *were* is a helpin' verb."

"Correct. Now, Mercy, did you pronounce each verb correctly?"

"Well, I guess not, considerin' I didn't add I-N-G to 'em. Want me to try it again?"

"Certainly."

"All right, here goes. I said you were talk-*ing* to us about not add-*ing* I-N-G to our verbs."

Well, I don't like how uppity I sound. Why, it sounds so fake, so...well, so uppity! I sound jist like my Yankee stepwitch! Well, maybe not exactly like her, but purty close.

"Okay, class, did you hear the clear enunciation of the verbs that time? Let's practice using I-N-G on these sentences...out loud, everyone."

Mrs. Reid proceeded to write the sentences on the blackboard. As each sentence was presented to the group, the class read aloud in unison. Over and over again.

Ok, I get the idea. She's tryin' to make us into somethin' we're not, shape us into those uppity Richmond folks—or worse, Yankees.

Following the lecture, Mrs. Reid presented her assignment.

"What I'd like for you to do is make every effort to enunciate the I-N-G on your verbs for the next week. In school, at home, and during conversations with friends throughout the day. As you become cognizant of the way you've dropped those sounds, you'll become more comfortable in catching yourself as you make mistakes. Then you can stop mid-sentence and enunciate the verbs correctly. Keep a running log of the number of times you catch yourself omitting the I-N-G on your verbs."

Oh, boy. I'm gonna sound ridiculous at home. I might jist give it a try at school, but no way am I gonna sound uppity around my kinfolk in Back Valley!

As if a telepathic message had been hurled in her direction, Mrs. Reid glanced at Mercy and added, "I know some of you will feel uncomfortable attempting this assignment, but you must give it a concerted effort. You will be graded heavily; it will be counted as a major test."

Darn teachers! Always comin' up with some kinda crap jist

to make you look downright stupid. Crap, crap, crap. I like the sound of that word. Crap, crap, crap. I know it's a bad word, maybe even worse than my other favorite word, shit, but I can't think of a better time to think it. As soon as I'm outa this class, I'm gonna say it out loud, jist say it right out loud, right there in the hallway.

The bell rang and Mercy scurried past her classmates. Taking a deep breath in the fresh air outside the hallway, she chanted, "Crap, crap, crap!"

There, I done it. I don't even care if I get in trouble, and I can't remember ever gettin' in trouble at school. Well, except maybe for talkin' too much.

Diligent about completing assignments, especially for Mrs. Reid, Mercy documented the number of times she failed to add I-N-G to her verbs. Uncomfortable with the assignment, Mercy battled the difficult task of altering the method in which she spoke.

As she tallied the mistakes and slips of the tongue while using verbs, Mercy logged each incident, even at home, the one place she dreaded the most as being seen different. But she was determined not to appear out of the ordinary with her neighbors.

They wouldn't understand. I know they'll likely see me as tryin' to become uppity, and I can't risk that. Wouldn't risk it, not even for an assignment for Mrs. Reid. Besides, I worked hard after movin' back from Detroit to fit in again around Back Valley, and the risk of bein' seen as different was...well, it would be too hurtful.

With total disregard to the assignment, Mercy continued to be true to herself, dropping as many I-N-Gs as she could. And convinced herself the assignment was of little significance in her life.

As Mercy suspected, she had compiled the largest number of dropped I-N-Gs of any student in her class. But at least she'd remained true to herself, and she felt satisfied. Mercy couldn't understand how simple words could make a difference in her life. After all, words are just words, she thought.

But Mercy would come to realize how powerful one single word could be.

CHAPTER 33

STICKS N' STONES

At the ripe age of 15, Mercy yearned to take part in all that her community and school had to offer, like the other teenagers. The school dances, basketball games and pajama parties had become an ever-growing source of friction at home; dating was always a bone of contention.

Mercy recalled the last battle with her granny about the subject. Although she had dated in the past, it had been a major battle with her granny each time.

"But I jist wanna go to the dance. I don't understand. Why can't I?"

"You're too young, and you ain't goin' to. Now hursh!"

Although certain that more pleas would only serve to enflame the battle, Mercy stood true to her nature and stubbornly persisted. She argued, "But everyone else my age dates. There ain't nothin' wrong with a boy takin' me to a dance at school. I don't understand."

"I don't believe in them dances nohow. They're against my Baptist beliefs. I said you ain't a-goin'! Now hursh!"

Shucks. I been down this road before. Always arguin' about attendin' school doin's and datin'. I'll jist call my daddy and see if he'll help me change Granny's mind.

"I wanna call my daddy in Michigan. You don't let me go nowhere! I'm a good girl. I ain't gonna do nothin' wrong." And without further thought of the consequences, Mercy quickly added, "Call Daddy. I bet he'll understand."

"Well, he ain't gonna let you go nowhere neither. Besides, you're under my care and I'll tell you what to do! And if'n you don't like it, I'll send you to that orphanage in Grundy!"

Like an overperfumed body, the biting words lingered in the air. The two opponents faced off in yet another skirmish in their never-ending battle.

Mercy sensed she was treading into dangerous territory with her granny.

But it don't matter no way. If I'm good, it's not ever good enough. So why not jist be that bad, sassy girl Granny always says I am? Sassy, sassy, always sassy. I reckon I shoulda jist been named Sassy; yeah, I like it.

As she shifted sideways to face her granny one more time, Mercy's pouting lips softened and a devilish smile spread across her face. "Well, call Daddy then!" she yelled.

Tired of the frustrating battle, Granny quickly grabbed up the phone, untwisted the cord and dialed R.C.'s long distance number in Detroit. Granny was determined to settle this argument; it was a test to see whose will would be the stronger.

But Mercy, too, was resolved. She wouldn't lose *this* battle.

Jist like the times I refused to chop off them chicken heads and wouldn't milk them cow tits. I ain't gonna give in.

Mercy overheard her granny's hateful end of the conversation, but she couldn't hear her daddy's response. As it usually did, Mercy's mind drifted far away from the dialogue, as it had been unconsciously trained to do. She'd heard her granny's unkind words spoken about her far too many times. *It's jist easier to ignore them*, she thought. It was far easier for the mind to drift away to a place of peaceful tranquility, a survival technique Mercy had adopted over time.,

"Well, I can't do a thing with her!" Granny shouted into the phone. "She's just so sassy; you know I can't take it no more! I feed her, clothe her, put a roof over her head…"

All the while, Mercy's mind continued its travels to mysterious, unknown places: places she'd discovered while reading books—fields of yellow buttercups, thick, green-blanketed forests, and huge, ancient oak trees with moss-coated roots. Tranquil visual imagery eased her mind and shielded Mercy's heart from pain.

Handing over the phone to Mercy, Granny snorted, "Well, here he is. Now ask 'im!"

Startled, Mercy looked up at her granny and smiled—then corrected her expression to present a more acceptable, solemn look.

Don't wanna count my chickens before they hatch. I jist know daddy's gonna convince Granny. Besides, I'm a grown girl and need to be allowed to go to town, visit friends, and date.

"Hi, Daddy! How're y'all doin' up North? And how's my brother Gary Wayne?"

"Well, all right, I reckon. But what in the worlds goin' on down there?" R.C. said.

Mercy detected a slight slur in his voice.

It's a weekend. Uh oh, he must be drinkin' as usual. I hope not; I need him to have a clear head this time. I need his full attention.

"Daddy, Granny won't let me go nowhere, not nowhere!" Mercy pleaded, then softened her voice, giving it a whiny tone.

"Well, I've already talked to her, and she ain't givin' in. You know how she is. You'd just as well set your mind to it. She ain't lettin' you date! And I'm up here in Detroit. There jist ain't nothin' I can do from up here."

"But, Daddy, I ain't gonna be doin' nothin' wrong. I jist wanna be like everybody else at school and go to dances." She added, "I'll be good. I promise."

"Well, you're jist gonna be another little whore—jist like your mother, Nell!"

Silence. Dead silence. Mercy dropped the phone with the cord still tangled in her hand.

Mercy felt the blood drain from her face. It followed the long, winding path into her arteries and veins, then into the capillaries, and finally to the hidden depths of her heart. A void had suddenly developed in her very being, one that would likely never be filled. Her spirit was shattered.

With total disregard for the bed linen, Mercy dropped the phone right in the middle of the yellow, chenille bedspread. As if in a trance, she retraced her earlier steps across the linoleum cracks in the sitting room, crossed the threshold into the living room, and silently moved through the doorway toward her refuge.

Without conscious volition, Mercy's legs moved her through the lot and across the wooden bridge, then carried her to the old barn. Hot tears stung her eyes as she opened the loft door and made her way to the hay bales. Moving farther to the back of the barn, she located the tiny space she had long ago crafted for herself. Hidden among the stacked bales was her secret hidey-hole, a space just large enough to tuck herself into snugly. It was one of her favorite places to retreat to when she was sad. She needed to give more thought to her daddy's spiteful words, and to hide without fear of being found by her granny. As a younger child, she had carried Teddy into the loft, and mourned with him in her arms. She still missed Teddy.

For hours, Mercy thought about her daddy's hurtful comment and ignored her granny's shrill yells. She wanted to stay hidden until she could resolve her conflicting emotions. For the first time in her life, Mercy questioned each memory, each story her daddy had shared with her about her mother.

How could he be so cruel, so hurtful? I know he was drinkin', but that ain't no excuse. I've seen him hit my stepmother, and I remember how he treated my mother. Maybe my mother had a reason to leave my daddy. I reckon he really can be a mean person. And I know he's an alcoholic. Ain't no denyin' the truth now.

Afterward, Mercy began the process of accepting a different perspective of her daddy—and herself. Even when she'd been younger, she realized her child-like adoration of him had been unwavering. Admittedly, she was responsible for the creation of the unrealistic image of her father. But she would no longer cleave to that image. Mercy accepted the fact that her father was flawed, and that she had been wrong to deny it before.

On this day, Mercy lost her unwavering, unconditional love for her father.

CHAPTER 34

LAUGH-IN

By the 10th grade year, begging to date and attend social events had exacerbated the tension at home. But Mercy was a teenager, a child of the '60s, and she hungered to emulate her peers. She dressed the same, even with the purchases at the Jot 'Em Down Store, and acted the same—but inside, she knew she was different.

Mercy knew there was no turning back now. In the near future, she would definitely be leaving Back Valley. By what means, she didn't know. But her future was as uncertain now as it had always been. Nothing had changed.

Don't I try to let Granny know I'm a good girl? Don't she realize I try to do my best in school? Don't she recognize I work hard at home to start them early mornin' fires, even since Dar-

rell got back from Detroit? Besides, Darrell ain't much good at chores since he's gone most of the time courtin' and hitchikin' the roads here and yonder between Cleveland and Lebanon, and doin' God knows what. So, I jist keep on sloppin' the hogs, choppin' the wood, and cleanin' the house. And anythin' else Granny might ask me to do. Well, except for milkin' them cows. And choppin' off them chicken heads on the choppin' block. I'm still mad as a hornet 'bout eatin' my pet chicken, when Granny cooked it for Sunday dinner.

For several years now, the television hadn't functioned, so Mercy had limited knowledge about up-to-date news, movies or music. Even a simple conversation at school with her friends often led to embarrassing remarks. She recalled the most recent conversation with her friends Freddie and Mike. It still smarted, just as if it had been yesterday.

"Wow, did y'all see that woman on TV last night? She was hilarious!" said Freddie. And Mike joined in with a hearty whoop and holler, "Yeah, she's cool, ain't she!"

Uh-oh, they must be talkin' about one of them new TV shows. Now how am I gonna bluff myself outa this one? Phew, gotta be more careful about them TV shows. I'd die from embarrassment if anybody besides Barbara Ann knows I don't have a television.

As was typical, Mercy tried hard to follow the conversations about television shows, praying she could provide the right response without divulging her secret: that she didn't own a TV, or even a radio.

"Ah, yeah, sure, which woman?" Mercy asked.

Freddie said, "You know, silly, the one with the long, blonde hair. The one with that ridiculous voice...Goldie, Goldie Hawn. Boy, ain't she sexy! And that joke she told had everybody in my house laughin', even my mom!" Freddie didn't guffaw like most boys; a sheepish grin spread across his mischievous face. Mike just stood there, waiting for Mercy's response, eager to retell the naughty joke.

"Of course, I saw her," Mercy lied. "And yeah, I guess you could say she's sexy, but you're a boy, remember; you think everythin' is sexy—and that goes for you, too, Mike." She forced a laugh, a concerted effort to sway her friends toward another subject.

"Well, what'd you think about that knock-knock joke?" Freddie said.

Frustrated she hadn't been able to change the subject by now, Mercy said, "What knock-knock joke?"

"Did you even see *Laugh-In*?" Mike asked.

Without thinking, Mercy blurted, "Well, it depends. What's *Laugh In*?" And she realized it was too late to take back her words.

Freddie and Mike simply stared at her, a long pause indicating their confusion.

Realizing she'd been unable to squeeze past their probing questions, Mercy tried to salvage the rest of the conversation. She'd almost let the secret slip.

"Ah, come on, guys, of course I did!" She lied, then added, "Come on, we're gonna be late for class, let's go." Mercy headed quickly toward the hallway. Without further questions, Freddie and Mike, like most other boys, followed her.

By now her body was in full blossom, but she considered herself a plain girl, perhaps even homely. She remembered how her aunts had repeatedly said, "You need to get that stringy hair cut." Her long, dark-brown hair now glowed with chestnut-auburn highlights, a muted mix attributed to her mother, Nell. The highlighted strands softened the roundness of her youthful face, yet made it impossible to hide her uncharacteristically large, deep-set brown eyes. Her youthful, curvy body was average, she guessed, but she adorned it well with her Jot 'Em Down clothes and shoes.

During that year, Mercy had felt unable to shake a deep-seated sense of unrest. As a volcano simmers and spews before its impending eruption, she felt it in the innermost fiber of her being, sensed it festering inside her gut, seething and fuming at her granny's biting comments. No matter how hard she tried, she would never please her granny. She wondered if maybe she was incapable of pleasing anyone. As tree limbs reach upward further and further from the roots anchoring them to the soil, Mercy's soul drifted bit by bit away from her beloved home. She spent her days ruminating about what her future might hold.

Mercy had always been at a loss to understand her granny's ever-present anger. Although sharing the same roof and the same meals, they shared little else. There would never be a family closeness, not even a hint of togetherness in their grandmother-granddaughter relationship. Finally, Mercy realized it had been doomed since the beginning, since she was five years old and had first come to live with her grandparents. She now longed to separate herself from the dread that everyday life presented her. For the first time she could ever recall, Mercy yearned to abandon Back Valley.

Of course, it had always been the *place* she had loved, not the home itself.

Constant arguments with her granny deepened her depression. Her interest in schoolwork waned as daily thoughts turned to running away.

But where would I go? What would I do? There's simply nowhere to go. I jist ache for a new beginnin'. Anywhere. I been in so many different homes through the years. Why would anyone want me now?

CHAPTER 35

TRUTH

Desperation takes various forms in one's life. When an injured bird in flight wraps its wings around itself and flies without direction, all sense of navigation becomes impaired. Hopefully with the passage of time, the will to survive takes precedence over its injury, and both body and mind intertwine to prevail.

Mercy realized she needed help and sought the aid of the one professional available, the one teacher in school who had been trained to help those in need. And so, Mercy began a routine of weekly visits to Truth Fraley, the school guidance counselor.

She loved that name: Truth…Truth…Truth. A lot can be said about a person's name, she thought. A woman named Truth. The name itself beckoned her, welcomed her presence. Somehow, the name brought a sense of peace, a sense of direction. And Mercy yearned to feel protected, to feel safe from the world. Truth—Mrs. Fraley—gave her that.

"But Mrs. Fraley, I don't know what to do. Granny slapped me again this mornin' right across the face with a magazine. I get so mad at her!"

Mrs. Fraley inquired, "Well, where did that happen?"

"In the kitchen, at home this mornin' before I left for school. See, my face is all red still. Here, look." And Mercy tilted her face to one side and traced her fingers outlining the imprint on her cheeks.

Mrs. Fraley stared at Mercy's reddened face, but averted her eyes. "Mercy, what do you think you need to do?"

"Well, I'm tired of it! Tired of bein' slapped. It happened twice last week, and I had handprints all day long on my face! I can't take it anymore, Mrs. Fraley, I just can't take…" And Mercy halted the sentence in midair, stared across Mrs. Fraley's desk and gazed out the office window.

Truth scrutinized Mercy's eyes, those prominent brown eyes that were so characteristic to other Musick children. She observed Mercy's pupils as they enlarged, watched the eyelids sweep upward to her brow and then downward. Then no movement. Just large, sad eyes, and that vacant, catatonic stare she had become accustomed to seeing. Moments of silence passed. Truth waited for a response, a typical counselor's method to elicit dialogue. Sometimes there was an awkward silence, but it was an effective technique.

Conscious avoidance…a defensive mechanism for maintaining self-control…reducing interaction, reducing anger. Give her time to compose herself. She needs time to reconcile and process her feelings. I need to help this child.

Truth simply stared at the broken child in front of her. During her role as both teacher and counselor, she had worked with several abused children. She was familiar with that stare, that blank expression void of emotion: minds elsewhere, as if drawn into an autistic world. It would be a short silence, Truth knew; she was aware Mercy was still mourning the loss of her childhood. But Truth had another concern.

What am I to do with this student? How can I help her? What plan of action should I take? And how will administration support me in my decision?

Mercy had been visiting consistently in the past few months. Truth sensed—no, she was certain—Mercy was depressed, perhaps clinically, and felt alone in her struggles at home. Abandonment issues from the loss of her mother, unresolved pain, inability to trust—all symptomatic of children who experience numerous caretakers in childhood. Mercy would likely self-destruct, but in what manner, Truth was uncertain. During her many sessions with Mercy, Truth had learned this student had lived in 14 separate homes during her fifteen years.

She knew Mercy had been forced to grow up far too quickly for a child's own emotional survival. Her defense mechanisms were transparent; she had learned that strong self-reliance and self-preservation were necessary for coping with the uncertainties of life.

Perhaps it was the right time, the appropriate moment to reveal what she had been planning. As a trained counselor, Truth recognized Mercy needed intervention. It was time to broach the subject of Mercy's leaving home, for her own emotional well-being. But she would patiently wait out this strained silence until Mercy was comfortable interacting again and ready for further dialogue. She needed to wait until Mercy was finished reliving the morning's "tapes" in her head and reviewing the most recent hurtful events at home.

Truth glanced downward at her cluttered desk. Her eyes moved from left to right as she reread the article in her latest counseling magazine, *More Stories from Adult Survivors of Childhood Trauma.*

My heart pounds just thinking about my childhood days. Physical and mental abusiveness truly destroyed my self-worth, at a very early age. I have spent my adult years trying to overcome a powerful grip of fear and frustration that never lets me go. Even today, years later, I find myself sometimes still angered at the question of why no adult anywhere, aware of my home life circumstances, ever helped me to escape from so many years of agony. How can a child be expected to endure such senseless abuse? How long did they think a day was for me, or a year, or my entire childhood? So many knew, but no one ever helped. They came, they heard, they saw, they pitied and they left. I am always tormented by the memories of that child who never found peace.

Truth's comment ended the silence. "Mercy, I've given your situation a great deal of thought. How would you feel about leaving home to live with another family? I'd make all the arrangements, and..."

Mercy broke in with a hopeful voice, "You mean I could actually *leave* Granny's?"

"Yes, I think I could help make that happen."

"How?"

"Well, I've been thinking. I know a family who could use your help, and I think they may be willing to provide a home for you in exchange for help with their children."

"You mean like a live-in babysitter? Where do they live? Could I finish high school here?" The last question ended in a desperate, pleading tone.

"Exactly. The woman's a teacher. Her name is Janette, and she and her husband own a local grocery store. They have two small children. With their business and full-time jobs, they're busy people. They could really use your help. And, yes, you'd still be able to graduate from Cleveland High School."

That's like music to my ears. Graduate at Cleveland High; no more new schools to get used to, no more new teachers, or new friends.

"But what'll Granny say?"

Truth already knew the answer. *Nothing.* But having already considered the question, she responded without hesitation, "Well, I've already talked to her about it. I didn't want to discuss it with you until I consulted with my boss and with your granny one more time."

Although Mercy already knew the answer, she asked, "And what'd Granny say?"

"Well, it's okay with her if it's okay with you. And your father is primary custodian; he would have to sign the paperwork, giving permission for you to move to another home."

Another home. Here we go again...

As simple as that, Mercy left Back Valley. But this time for good.

CHAPTER 36

LIVIN' IN
A MANSION

Mercy cautiously approached her new home on Mill Creek for the first time, and halted at the ivy-draped rock steps outside the decorative iron gate. She stood there a moment in wonder as she looked at her new surroundings. It was, indeed, an impressive home. Or it was in its heyday, she thought. She gazed upward, her eyes following the outline of the old home. An imposing structure, the red brick two-story house faced an abandoned gristmill, Jessee's Mill, located directly across Mill Creek Road. Atypical in both setting and façade, the exterior of the home was a stark contrast to most homes in the surrounding area. Although in deplorable condition, white pillars surrounded the main porch.

Mercy took note of the supporting pillars, as well as the front porch in various stages of disrepair—rotting floorboards, peeling paint and a sinking foundation. Tall, narrow, interlocking wooden doors welcomed visitors into the grand entrance of the hallway.

These people must be rich, rich, rich. Why, I ain't never been in such a big house! Look at that fancy woodwork, the high ceilings...and that chandelier! I musta died and gone to heaven. God must've answered my prayers. Lord, I promise not to be sassy and to work even harder in this new home.

The old Jessee home was unlike anything Mercy had seen in her 15 years. A large parlor room accented with a prominent bay window awaited guests as they entered the front hallway. A smaller, more informal room, the den, was located across the hallway; it adjoined an even larger dining area. Although decorated modestly, a massive oak dining table was centered in the room, which allowed 10 diners to be seated at a meal. A comfortable, small kitchen was located in the rear of the home. A second story featured three oversized bedrooms, each boasting its own private fireplace.

A home with two bathrooms! Mercy reveled in the magnificence of such splendor. She was, indeed, lucky to be alive. For the first time in many years, she was thankful for her existence, and her new station in life.

I sure do love this family's color television. Now I can keep up with all my friends 'bout the latest TV shows, especially Laugh-In. *And not feel so poor.*

Mercy enjoyed learning about the history of Mill Creek, specifically the old gristmill. With a view from her very own bedroom, she often stared at the imposing three-story structure, pondering about the Jessee family that once lived in the old home, and who had used the gristmill across the roadway. On lazy Sunday afternoons, she often made the short trip out the front porch, down the rock steps, across the wooden bridge, and into the mill, exploring for hours. Meticulously peering into each nook and cranny inside the building, she felt certain she had examined every square inch. Most of all, she admired the abandoned milling machines left inside the old structure and the huge outside water wheel. A small waterfall near the old mill's dam provided her a refreshing dip into cool mountain water during the hottest summer days.

At last, she felt content with her life. Chores at the new home became pleasurable. Babysitting the children, cleaning the large home, and washing and ironing clothes became a routine—but she took pleasure in her new responsibilities.

Mercy adored the two children left in her charge. Content with her newfound life, she was attentive and amused by the rambling, make-believe stories of the five-year-old girl, Alice, and the consistently playful antics of the older boy, Mike.

What lucky children they are, to have two parents that love 'em, that provide for 'em—all without complaints that they are too much trouble, too much work, or they eat too much food. And without the threat of bein' sent to an orphanage in Grundy.

Slowly, and without conscious recognition, a sense of peaceful security eventually enveloped Mercy's heart and soul. She was ready to trust again.

I reckon I'll finally be all right.

Mercy knew she wasn't loved by them in a familial way, but they treated her with respect. With a renewed sense of hope and purpose, she began to dream about her future, a future that included a treasured college education, and one final move from the area.

She learned that her younger siblings, Joyce and Randy, had not been as fortunate as she had been. Likely tired of dealing with children, Nell's mother, Josie, had sent them from her home in Bluefield, it seemed. It appeared Nell had left them in Josie's care for an extended period of time and Josie had simply grown tired of the only two grandchildren left in her care.

How could her grandmother, Josie, be so cruel? And where is my mother? Didn't she care? How could she! I'll never forget the day she left me. Please don't leave me! Will I ever be able to forget those words?

For one unforgettable night, Joyce visited Mercy at the old mansion on Mill Creek. Two sisters reunited, they shared stories about living in foster homes, laughed uncontrollably at silly jokes, and discussed their mother, Nell.

"Why'd she send you away?" asked Mercy.

Without hesitation, as if she were somehow protecting the reputation of her mother, Joyce said, "Well, she really didn't. It was Grandma Josie."

Mercy could relate to the strange behaviors of grandparents. "Where was Nell?" She found it difficult to call the woman her mother.

After all, she hadn't ever been a real mother. Gave us all up like we were stray kittens. Besides, I like callin' her by her first name: Nell.

It was an act of empowerment to call her mother by her first name. An act of rebellious disrespect.

"Well, I reckon she was off on one of them drinkin' trips, you know. Sometimes, she'd leave for a week or two at a time and leave me and Randy with Grandma Josie."

"Where would she go?" Mercy asked.

"Don't know. Just off somewhere. Maybe with Ray."

Mercy remembered Ray. The pock-faced stepfather.

Well, not a stepfather. Not really. Nell didn't marry him, so

I reckon he was just a boyfriend, really. I didn't like his strange behaviors. Didn't trust him. I found out why I didn't wanna leave Joyce in Bluefield. Wish I hadn't asked so many darn questions. And I don't like the fact my sister is livin' in a foster home, too. But what could they do?

Throughout that special night, Mercy delved into her sister's past. She questioned Joyce over and over again about her experiences while living in various states throughout the country: somewhere in California; witnessing racial riots in Detroit; Augusta, GA; Orlando, FL; and on and on. Joyce revealed details about different schools, strange neighbors, and even more eccentric behaviors exhibited by Nell *and* Ray.

Later, Mercy chastised herself for becoming too comfortable living in her mansion on Mill Creek. Experience had taught her to remain guarded against complacency. And she was right to do so.

CHAPTER 37

THE BLUE-EYED BOY

"Touchdown for the Pioneers!" screamed the sports announcer.

Mercy shifted her body to survey the crowd while the fans reacted to the referee's final decision. It was her first football game; she watched as Lebanon High School Pioneer fans bounded into the air, feverishly waving red and white triangular-shaped banners through the standing-room-only crowd. Out on the field, Pioneer cheerleaders vaulted into the air, chanting, "Go Pioneers, go! Go Pioneers, go!" in front of the enthusiastic crowd. At the same time, the band joined in, trumping out lively music, providing an even more festive feel and carnival-like spirit to the event.

I jist can't help it. I hate this sport. Don't understand it one bit. Don't understand all them stupid rules and regulations. And I don't understand what all the fuss is 'bout. It's jist a game. Jist a silly old game. Boys runnin' around a field, chasin' a ball and kickin' it between two goal posts. Don't make no sense to me. Wish Cleveland High School'd had a team. Maybe I'd understand the game better if we'd had one. Oh, why'd my school have to be so small that it couldn't have a football team? I love basketball, though. Watched the Cleveland Indians play. But for the life of me, I can't understand this silly game of football. But, like everythin' else, I'll jist pretend I do. I reckon I'm purty good at pretendin'.

She needed to distance herself from the deafening roar of the football game, so Mercy turned and strolled away from the bleachers, back in the direction of the concession stands, beside her latest boyfriend from Lebanon High School, Herbert Burl. She found his sense of humor captivating, and his laughter infectious. But most importantly, his older-boy-lives-outside-my-town charm added to the overall mystique of why she was interested in him. At least for that week, or maybe for that month.

Hand in hand, they both concentrated on nudging through the elbow-to-elbow crowd, but paused when they heard, "Hey Hubby, where ye goin' so fast?" (Hubby was Herbert Burl's nickname.)

Turning to acknowledge the stranger, Mercy asked, "Well, who's this?" Awkwardly standing, shuffling her feet side to side as if she had to relieve her bladder, she listened to Hubby chatter with his friend, totally disregarding her presence. Mercy detested being ignored, but she listened to them joke and swap wisecracks with one another. Probably things only a boy could understand, she thought.

"Oh, you don't even wanna know who this guy is," said Hubby with a hearty laugh and a twinkle of mischievousness spread across his face.

"Well, I reckon I do," she said without thought. "Ain't you gonna introduce us?"

"All right. If you insist," said Hubby, again with a knowing smile for his friend. "This is T.J."

And as simple as that, Mercy was introduced to the most handsome boy she thought she'd ever met. Gazing into his intense, ice-blue eyes, she took note of his uncommonly long eyelashes, infectious smile, and overall good looks—and was instantly spellbound by his charm. Hypnotized, as if in a trance, she stood transfixed in that solitary moment in time. She awkwardly stammered, "Hi, I'm Mercy."

"Howdy, I'm T.J.," he said. As if it was an afterthought, and a further need to poke fun at his friend, he added, "What in the world are you doin' with this guy? Don't you know he's crazy?"

As the boys said goodbye, she tucked T.J. into the back of her mind, mentally compiling a list of reasons she was so attracted to this new boy. At this moment in time, Mercy had no inkling of how this one person would play such a significant role in changing her life.

CHAPTER 38

MOVIN' AGAIN

With perfect clarity, Mercy recalled the day her life was once again altered.

"Mercy, I need to talk to you," said Janette. "Could you come to the kitchen table?"

Taking note of Janette's serious tone, Mercy set aside her homework on the dining room table, sauntered into the kitchen, pulled out a metal chair and seated herself in front of Janette.

"Sure, I reckon I can take a break from all that homework." Mercy attempted a slight smile, a nervous gesture to prepare for what she perceived to be a more-than-normal serious conversation. She reflected upon her last few days at her home on Mill Creek; it had been a hectic time for everyone in the family, even the children. Janette had been admitted into Lebanon General

Hospital, and Mercy's chores had increased to meet the additional demands at home. Everyone had pitched in to help, even the small children and Janette's husband, Stan.

Taking note of the serious look on Janette's face, Mercy asked, "What's wrong? Did I do something wrong?" Her conditioned response rose to the surface: an I'll-do-anything-to-please-you response.

What could I have done? I don't think I did anythin' wrong while Janette was in the hospital. I tried extra hard around the house. Maybe I didn't clean the house good enough. Or I didn't iron enough clothes last week. I know my cookin' wasn't very good. Janette's an excellent cook. Maybe Stan didn't like my gravy an' biscuits I made this mornin'. Oh, please don't let it be anythin', at least not anythin' big.

Janette said, "Mercy, I've been sick lately."

"I know. Are you feelin' better?" She responded with genuine concern in her voice.

"Well, yeah, I am, but…" And she paused mid-sentence before adding, "I need to make some decisions."

Now Mercy knew the conversation would be of a more serious nature than she had hoped. "What kinda decisions?" she probed, keenly aware that somehow her own future would be involved in this uncomfortable conversation.

As if lecturing in her teacher-like voice, Janette said, "Mercy, I talked with my doctor, and he feels I'm under way too much stress, and that I need to alleviate some of the stress in my life." She averted her eyes from Mercy's gaze.

"Stress?"

So, I must be a part of that stress? I had no idea Janette was stressed any more than the rest of us. What in the world did I do to cause stress? I thought I was helpin' here. It don't make no sense to me.

"Yes, I'm going to have to ask you to leave." And then Janette quickly added, "I've already spoken with your Uncle Lawrence on two occasions—and he has agreed to take you to Narrows to live with him."

Mercy's mouth gaped wide as a string of emotions ripped inside her. She spluttered, "But whaddaya *mean* I have to *leave?!*" She noticed how the last word elevated as it sluiced past her lips— maybe too much. Guardedly, she lowered her tone. More than anything, she didn't want to appear out of control. Or disrespect-ful to Janette, she thought. She listened as her bowels churned from her latest meal and a voice inside her screamed, *not another move—not again!*

This latest revelation was unemotional. Factual. Unyielding.

Attempting to hide her tears, Mercy's shoulders drooped as she molded her posture into a more subservient position. She lowered her gaze. "But what'll I do about graduatin' from school? You mean I gotta move again? To Narrows? Change schools durin' my senior year?" she asked. The words tumbled haphazardly from her lips.

I must've been too sassy...no, that can't be it. I worked hard at not talkin' back to Janette and her husband. That can't be it! I can't even remember one time when I've been disrespectful. Un-wanted. That must be it. That was always it. I tried so hard *here in this new home. No one ever wants me for very long. Unwant-ed. Unwanted. Unwanted! It's always been that way. It'll never change.*

There would be no need to argue. Or beg. The decision had already been made.

In a blind stupor, Mercy gathered her personal belongings, stuffed them inside brown paper bags, and then called her cousin

Nancy in Back Valley. "Could you come get me?" she pleaded. In between tears, she explained, "They want me to leave. I jist can't believe it. I don't know what else to do. But I don't wanna go live in Narrows."

While she waited for her cousin, hot tears stung Mercy's eyes as they roamed around the bedroom she had learned to cherish so dearly. She would miss this special room, this space where she'd spent hours studying, reading and relaxing. Her very own balcony door that she had opened to provide light and fresh air into her room. The oversized window where she had spent hours gazing onto the old Jessee's Mill. The fireplace, although no longer used, which had given her so much comfort and pride. She was more than devastated, more than heartsick, and more than disappointed in herself. *I must have done something wrong*, she thought.

Her last phone call was to T.J., her new boyfriend. "I'm packed. I'm leavin' for Back Valley. I'll be stayin' with my cousin Nancy for a while. You can call me there."

Mercy was desperate now, and unsure how she'd complete her senior year at Cleveland High School—and attend college in the near future. But she promised herself she would do it somehow.

Her dreams were obliterated again. Shattered beyond despair and like a forest creature caught in a raging, inescapable fire, she blindly navigated the next few days at school as if in a fog. A dream turned into a nightmare, trapped with no way out.

What'll I do now? Where will I stay until the end of this school year? How will I finish my senior year at Cleveland High School? Who would want me?

One night during a conversation with T.J. on the phone, he said, "Well, I reckon we'll just run away and get married."

The problem is solved! Now I won't be sent to Michigan to

live with the stepwitch again, or be sent to Narrows. I can't go back to Back Valley at Granny's again. Mrs. Fraley can't help me this time; I've got nowhere else to go. And, besides, the only person who ever loved me is T.J. And I love him. Hasn't he always wanted me? Hasn't he always told me he loved me?

Mercy and T.J. married in September of her senior year. Two weeks later, it was her 17th birthday.

CHAPTER 39

FOLLOWIN' IN NELL'S FOOTSTEPS

Like a giant oak tree, roots meandered, spread out, and dug deeply into the integral parts of Mercy's life. She was a part of Appalachia, a place where the spirit of individualism and self-reliance were all-encompassing. Like others around her, she took pride in her stubbornness in not wanting to be beholding to others; in her love of living in the mountains; in the desire to encourage families who left the area to not forget their roots, and to come back home; in the sense of humor among people to make fun of themselves, yet be fiercely unappreciative of outsiders who made fun of their dialect; in the concept of being yourself and not putting on airs or getting above your raising; in the innate sense of not trusting outsiders and strangers; and in the sense that blood runs thicker than water. Those were the things Mercy wanted and valued most.

In her world, she knew it was acceptable, sometimes expected, for girls to marry at a younger age. That pioneer heritage of Appalachian women had certainly been passed onto her, since these same traits flowed deeply within her veins. The same characteristics that had enabled her mother and other women to endure adversity had taught her to be strong and resilient. She'd be no different; I'll survive, too, she thought.

But Mercy did fight against the fatalistic approach to life, the sense that outside forces would control her destiny. The sense that other girls like her living in the mountains were subjugated to the power of the male, defined in terms of their readiness for marriage. Her granny's emphasis on domestic housekeeping chores on the farm had been essential for her to be considered a good wife. For the most part, a formal education for women was viewed as insignificant. Getting married and bearing children had been her forebears' means for securing an identity and stability. She would control her own destiny in these matters, she promised herself.

More than once, Mercy had read articles about the third-world nation which some believed existed in her Appalachian Mountains, her homeland and birthplace. Like most of her relatives, she had ignored all the attention in newspapers, magazines and on television. LBJ's War on Poverty had, indeed, brought unwanted attention to the women in Appalachia. But with fervor, she'd read, listened, and absorbed this information. Mercy had already determined she would not become another statistic.

As these thoughts rambled inside her head, Mercy remembered the magazine article she had carefully tucked away inside her purse. Reaching down deep, she pulled out the crumpled paper, smoothed the edges and began to read the excerpt from the research paper "Too Young to Wed" by Mathur, Greene, and Malhotra. This time, she read it aloud to herself.

"Early marriage contributes to a series of negative consequences both for young girls and the societies in which they live. The timing of early marriage almost always disrupts girls' education, reducing their opportunities for future financial independence through work. Young women are often married without autonomy or decision-making power. This relative lack of power is associated with higher levels of violence in marriage and higher rates of divorce. Early marriage is more common in the Appalachian region than it is in richer and more developed settings. There is an overall lack of opportunity, skills, and social support for young girls, as compared to boys. Young girls are least likely to benefit from educational and economic policies and programs. Parents are often less interested in investing in the education of daughters because the benefits of their investment will be lost. After marriage, young married girls' access to formal education is severely limited because of a lack of mobility, domestic burdens, childbearing, and social norms that view marriage and schooling as incompatible. Since early marriage limits skills, resources, knowledge, social support, mobility, and autonomy, young married girls often have little power in relation to their husbands or in-laws. They are also extremely vulnerable to violence, abuse, divorce, and abandonment. Violence may include physical, sexual, psychological, and economic abuse. Nobody protests against early marriage because daughters are seen as a burden."

Mercy reflected upon the possible consequences of her early marriage to T.J. She recalled that no one, not *one* family member had discouraged her from getting married. No one had warned her about the ramifications of marrying at such a young age; no one offered advice about attending college; and no one suggested any reason for her to wait until the end of her senior year. What were they thinking? She had, indeed, been a burden to her family, or they would have rescued her from herself.

She did, however, recall how her English teacher, Mrs. Reid, had voiced disappointment at her decision to get married. Like a church tower bell ringing over a small town and demanding an audience, her words would ring and haunt Mercy throughout the years: "Mercy, do you realize what you have done?!"

Mercy had conflicting emotions. Perhaps it was fate, those outside forces controlling my life, she thought. But she had, indeed, followed in her mother Nell's footsteps. The thought disappointed her. But as she had done in the past, she accepted that she was where she was supposed to be in life.

CHAPTER 40

CORN VALLEY

Like a Vesuvian volcanic eruption, Mercy's innards boiled and fissure-type explosions blasted toxic thoughts inside her head. Thoughts that spewed steam, smoke and lethal gases, then belched them onto her surrounding exterior. Violent explosions blasted clouds of gas-laden debris into the air around her. Large quantities of lava disabled everything in her path. Such was Mercy's epiphany.

She had, indeed, made a mistake to marry so young. But she was reluctant to mention that fact to anyone; it was difficult to admit it, even to herself. She promised not to mention it to her husband, at least for now.

The incessant questions concerning which boys she had talked to during the school day frustrated her. T.J.'s possessive jealousy and out-of-control temper confused her. He didn't want anyone else to notice her. She couldn't smile too long or too much with another boy, not even her best male friends at school. He didn't like her joking too much, or talking too long with other boys.

Her initial reaction had been one of flattery. She was flattered that someone loved her so. Flattered that someone cared enough to be concerned about her. But in time, she realized it was not flattery. Mercy came to dread his questions and their conversations, and she learned to avoid direct, specific responses.

That nagging feeling never left her, that men were somehow better than women. That women were subservient and told what to do, what to say, and how to act.

Well, I won't accept it. I jist can't, and I jist won't. I'm way too stubborn. But what will I do? I've made my bed. I'll jist have to lay in it, I reckon. There ain't no way out now. I'll make the best of it. There ain't no goin' back. Just like my mother. And all the other young girls that got married before me. But I'll be different. I'll get that education. And someday...someday, I'll leave this area and never come back. I wanna live somewhere where women are treated as equals to men, treated with respect for what we know. Simply treated with respect, not as a second-class citizen. And never be expected to eat at a table after the men ate first. Never again.

With uncertainty about her future, Mercy moved in with T.J.'s parents in Corn Valley, into a tiny, unassuming home perched against the backdrop of majestic Beartown Mountain, one of the most scenic, isolated mountain peaks in the state. Even at lower elevations, rhododendron thickets and spruce trees could be spotted among the tree lines in the distance. At the foot of the mountain near Elk Garden, a dirt road gradually inclined, winding by Stuart-owned cattle farms, the old Stuart Company Store, the Loop Church of Christ, and eventually to Mercy's new home.

Tucked against a low bank, the small, white-siding home boasted a wide plank porch that faced the front road. A large blue spruce encroached onto one side of the porch, its top peaking above the roofline, its sides bulging. This provided a semblance of privacy for the family. But like in the past at her granny's house, Mercy preferred the open-ended section of the porch, which allowed her to wave at each car as neighbors passed to and fro on the seldom-traveled road.

Although comfortable in her new home, Mercy expressed concern to T.J. about their lack of privacy. The main door to the house led directly into the living room and gave a side view of their bedroom, even a glimpse of their bed

Oh, why can't they put up a door to this bedroom! Lord A' mercy; everybody can see everythin' in here, I reckon. Can't have a bit of privacy. Every single visitor, every neighbor, and all the kinfolks can see right into this bedroom. And T.J.'s daddy sets in his favorite chair and watches TV right here. Please put up a door to this room, please! Why, even T.J.'s sister walked in and caught me naked as a jaybird this mornin'. People jist comin' and goin' all day long, in and out of our bedroom. No privacy. Lord, help us!

But Mercy's prayers for a door to the bedroom went unanswered. There were more important things to consider, like finishing high school. Mercy and T.J. both pursued completing their senior year: T.J. at Lebanon High, and Mercy at Cleveland High. She was committed; he appeared disinterested. Each day overlapped into yet another, as homework and household chores kept growing. But Mercy was conditioned to hard work.

Most of all, she didn't want to become an additional burden to her new family. So, on each Monday's washday, Mercy stayed home from school to help her aging mother-in-law with laundry. As her absences mounted at school, her grades began to suffer for the first time since she had conquered those multiplication tables, and she had promised school would be a priority in her life.

Writing her own excuses for Monday's absences from school, each Tuesday she handed Miss Dotson the same note: "Please excuse my absence yesterday. I was helping with laundry at home."

How ridiculous it all seems now, and how ironic. The girl with all the dreams that are all gone now. I ain't done nothin' with my life. Nothin'. Until an opportunity comes in the future for me to redeem myself. And it will come. Somehow, I'll make it happen.

With her husband's approval, Mercy received her driver's license that year. A driver's license sanctioned by T.J., who signed for her since she was only 17 and not legally of age to drive. She was incensed, embarrassed, and humiliated. Old enough to be married, but not old enough to drive without her husband's signature.

Mercy watched T.J. struggle academically during the remainder of their senior year, managing time between helping his disabled father at the family's grocery store and time with his new wife. It was a daily challenge for both of them, Mercy realized. Each weekday afternoon, T.J. traveled on the school bus route to his family's grocery store in Belfast, while Mercy traveled another direction to Corn Valley. Chores and homework, compounded with the stress of being a newly married couple, presented new issues. But Mercy and T.J. were determined to make their marriage a success, and both recognized the importance of receiving their high school diplomas. They never wavered in this decision.

In preparation for their graduation, Mercy and T.J. spent their weekends studying for tests, completing projects, and finishing required homework. Near the end of the year, Mercy became concerned; she doubted T.J. would graduate high school that year—but he did. And she was ecstatic to be a 1970 graduate of Cleveland High School.

She clearly recalled the significance of her graduation night and driving the old hand-me-down station wagon—the one with the missing side window, with the cardboard taped over it to prevent the onslaught of the beating rain—on her own on graduation night.

Maneuvering the sharp, winding curves on Cleveland Mountain during heavy rain was challenging, even for the most seasoned driver. On that night, Mercy had cautiously approached each new bend, mindful of the closeness of each bank, and adjusted her headlight beams for a better view between oncoming cars. Her thoughts had transported her back to the location of her birth.

Right here, right here on this very mountain. Which curve? How'd Nell stand the pain? Is childbirth really all that painful?

In the headlights, an oncoming car grabbed Mercy's attention and she reminded herself to slow down and stay alert. As she passed by the curve where her life unceremoniously began, she glanced sideways. But the sheet of cardboard covering the missing window, soaked and darkened by the rain now, blocked her view. Unable to pull to the side of the road, or pause due to the pounding onslaught of rain and constraint for time, Mercy drove forward. She had passed this sight hundreds of times over the years, she reminded herself. This Friday night was no different. She had a greater mission to accomplish: marching in her high school graduation ceremony.

And she did.

But that proud moment seemed short-lived; on the following Monday morning, Mercy began work at the sewing factory.

CHAPTER 41

THE PETTICOAT FACTORY

Mercy moped sullenly as she walked through the factory's double doors at the rear of the red brick building with a frown on her face at 6:45 in the morning. She immediately reacted to the sounds already reaching her sensitive ears. The roaring *clickety, click, click* of the machines stressed her already. Without conscious thought, her body reacted. Arms and hands sagged downward toward the outline of her hips. Her lips tightened into a well-defined line and her narrow shoulders drooped; her body's posture unconsciously mimicked her feelings. Tiredness. Boredom. Defeat.

*Whirr…whirr…whirr…bzz…bzz…bzzz…*The relentless sounds of sewing machines were never-ending. The noisy drone of the machines smothered the air around her. Locating her time card, she picked it up, eyed it suspiciously, and stuck it into the machine. *Click-chunk.* Time and date were stamped across the upper right-hand corner.

"Hey, Mercy, how're ya doin' today?" Someone called.

Who is that person? Don't know, don't care. Jist get me through another day.

Without raising her head and with a forced smile, she responded, "All right, I reckon." And her feet propelled her farther into the building, closer to the center, closer to the dreaded machines and assembly lines.

The noxious smell of cleaning fluids permeated the air around her and teased her nostrils. Her nostrils flared outward, sucking in the dirty air filled with cotton lint from the previous day's work. Sucking it deeper and deeper into her lungs.

Glancing downward toward her shoes, she noticed a feeble attempt had been made to remove the residual effects of the materials from the floor space in front of her serger machine.

At 6:57, a bell rang warning employees to march to their respective machines and prepare for work. Again on cue, at 7:00, another bell. The floor supervisor yelled, "All right, everybody; let's get to work, now!"

Like robots, the workers sat before their machines, and conversation halted.

Mercy was accustomed and conditioned to bells: tardy bells to enter the classroom, bells to signal beginning of classes, bells to signal lunch time, and bells to signal the end of the school day.

Whirr...whirr...whirr... Same thing every day, day in, day out. Production was all important. You must make production on the production line if you want job security. Eight hours of work for wages of $1.50 per hour—without questions and without complaints.

Each day, Mercy felt fortunate she hadn't been forced to work overtime, like many of her co-workers. She'd quickly discovered the reason; it was illegal for the company to allow someone her age, at the age of 17, to work in excess of 40 hours per week.

"Well, why ain't *you* gonna work overtime today? I have to. Why don't they never ask *you*?" someone had asked.

"Oh, they can't make me work overtime. I ain't old 'enough."

For the past four months, she'd enjoyed bragging about her predicament each time the question had been presented to her. And at 3:30 each day, she'd practically danced in the air as she made her way to the back parking lot, abandoning all the other women who had no choice in the matter. They had no more choice about working the mandatory overtime than they did any other area of their lives.

Monotony. Repetition. First, sew halfway down the side of the slip, then tuck the size label into the remaining portion of the garment: small, medium, or large. Change bobbins. Change threads. Pick up the ticket. Put the ticket on your time sheet.

Mercy questioned everything. She was miserable, smothered, and claustrophobic.

Glancing sideways, but still expertly navigating the L-sized petticoat through the machine, she surveyed the other women in closest proximity to her. Rows of sewing machines were arranged like the classroom desks she was familiar with in school. The machines were spaced just far enough apart to allow each worker to work unhindered, to move in and out freely to pick up materials and carry their bundles to and fro, then flop the piles near their machines. And do it all over again…over and over.

Still bored but lost in thought, Mercy stretched her neck and shoulders forward for a better view of the front of the sewing floor. She saw her cousin Sissy expertly navigating the bar tack machine as she attached straps to the slips. Nearby was Sissy's sister, Nancy, whose job was to attach a fancy silk appliquéd medallion to the slips.

How many years have they both been here? Sissy more 'n 20, Nancy for 9... How do they do it? Day in, day out. Drivin' from Back Valley, even through the ice and snow in winters. Well, I ain't gonna do it. I'll never be that devoted to sewin' slips at this factory.

She glanced all around: to the right, to the left, and then behind her. People moved like robots, their tired facial expressions flat and emotionless. Rows of robotic workers hunched awkwardly over their machines, all surrounded by petticoats. With ulcer-inducing anxiety, Mercy glanced with dread at her machine. Her stack of petticoats loomed: her heaping piles, waiting for her to sew them.

How in the world did I get to this place? Will this be all there is to my life? And I don't really understand what production means. If you're already paid minimum wage, why'd you have to make production? I reckon it's jist another way of earnin' the pitiful salary they pay me. $1.50 an hour. And I wonder what would happen if I didn't make production? Would they take money from my $50-a-week paycheck? Would they fire me? Would they lay me off? Been here four months and still hate it! Well, I won't do it forever. I can't do it...well, not for long anyhow.

Mercy fought back the tears. Tears had already come that day, early that morning before work. Each day as she drove into the parking lot of the plant, she turned to T.J. in the car and sobbed.

"Do I have to go inside this miserable place? I hate it! I tell you, I'm about to puke!"

"Well, I reckon you don't have to if'n you don't want to. But we need the money."

And that was the end of it. She knew they needed money; they'd had no income and had lived solely on the generosity of her in-laws until they both had graduated high school.

She was miserable in this new role as an hourly laborer at the sewing plant, a non-union facility, but recognized her options were limited. At age 17, there were few choices for employment in the small town, especially for women.

Strict demands were placed on workers' time. Seven-minute breaks each morning. A 30-minute lunch. Seven-minute breaks in the afternoon.

Why, I had more freedom on the farm in Back Valley! At least I could roam around outside, talk to the cows n' pigs, kick a can down the road when I got bored. And not be forced to sit inside all day. Oh, how I miss the chance to breathe in that fresh mountain air. It makes me plumb ill just thinkin' about how everybody here works so hard. Jist like slaves, breakin' their backs sewin' all them fancy slips for companies and stores like Diane von Furstenberg and Saks Fifth Avenue, stores none of us will ever see. And clothes I'll never own like them rich people wear. Rich folks, outsiders, who buy them slips we work so hard to make.

But she and T.J. needed the money. She was married now, with new responsibilities. She had to accept her new role in life.

Mercy was jolted from her thoughts as the floor supervisor darted around the corner, halted at her row and then approached her machine. She stiffened involuntarily, as she always had in the past. She tired of supervisors walking up behind her, looming over her shoulder and timing her progress on a regular basis with their time clocks.

"Well, Mercy, we got overtime for ye today." Her floor supervisor said. Not a question, a demand. The bosses had arbitrary power over the workers.

Without pausing, Mercy smugly responded, "Oh, I can't work over. I ain't old enough." And she continued sewing the slip without giving her supervisor even the slightest glance upward to make eye contact.

"Oh, I heard you turned eighteen today. Ain't that right? It's your birthday?" the supervisor asked, a smug smile on her face.

"Yeah, it's my birthday, I reckon. How'd *you* know?" And she was immediately sorry for her flip response.

"Well, you can work overtime then? Ain't that right?"

And she did.

"Five Tiny Pink Fingers"
By K. Godbey

Five tiny pink fingers,
flailing to and fro
clinging to your hand
entwining your heart.
Five tiny pink fingers,
guiding your footsteps
keeping your grasp on life
holding tightly to memories.
Five tiny pink fingers
loving unconditionally
reminding you to love
even the unlovable
Five tiny pink fingers
saved my life.

CHAPTER 42

FIVE TINY PINK FINGERS

Glaring fluorescent lights blinked off and on and stung Mercy's eyes. She sensed movements in the background and heard mumbled voices, incoherent comments, and then laughter. Blinking intermittently to avoid the pain, Mercy became aware of muffled screams in the distance. Then a faint cry, and another, and another. Beyond the anesthetic fog, Mercy struggled to clear her mind. This was an important event. But the significance escaped her at the moment. Where was she? What had happened to her? And why did she continue to hear those unintelligible, garbled voices in the distance?

As if a giant hand had reached out to swish away the fog,

she remembered—with perfect clarity. She was in the birthing room at Johnston Memorial Hospital in Abingdon. Those were *her* screams. *Her* baby's cry.

"Well, tell me, what is it? Tell me. Is it okay?" She mumbled to no one in particular. And not waiting for a response, she added, "Is it a boy or a girl?"

She was just trying to locate anyone who was willing to respond to her muffled questions.

"Oh, it's a little girl," someone cooed in the distance.

"Well, is she okay? Let me see 'er," Mercy demanded.

"Be patient. We're cleanin' her up for you now," the seasoned nurse explained in a faraway, monotone voice. She spoke with practiced clarity and diction, as if this were an everyday event for her.

Without further delay, a nurse gently placed Mercy's newborn child upon her chest. And Mercy was in love, for the first time in her life. Mercy's love for this tiny being was a new type of love, far beyond anything she had experienced in her lifetime: the love a mother has for her offspring. Unconditional. Everlasting.

The word *love* kept repeating itself, over and over again in her head. Her heart fluttered as she recognized the instant maternal bonding she felt for her new baby.

What is that I'm feelin'? These new emotions! Did my mother feel like this when I was born in that truck on Cleveland Mountain? No, I can't imagine my mother feelin' the same way I do right now—or else she wouldn't have abandoned me. How could she? How could she leave somethin' so precious, so helpless, so innocent?

At that moment, Mercy compiled a list of reasons why she'd never leave *her* child, never abandon her to strangers. Never, ever. An old favorite song of hers, by Ricky Nelson, popped into her head and she silently hummed the lyrics: "Welcome to my world, come on in...."

Without question, Mercy promised her newborn she would do whatever was necessary to protect her from the unknown. She would fiercely protect her from those who sought to be unkind to her, and shelter her from those who wouldn't want her. Forever protected, forever wanted, she thought. What a novel concept.

Mercy professed that her child, without question, would now become the new focus in her life. This tiny figure, this tiny person, would become her new priority—above and beyond anything she could ever feel for T.J. Life as she had known it had become altered at that moment in time. She knew she would never be the same again.

Touching the edges of the pink blanket that had been placed upon her chest, Mercy pulled aside the folds of the material and looked at the toes, then the fingers. She counted them. Gingerly, she pulled the blanket away from the entire tiny body, and looked at this new gift God had given her.

All the while, a nurse lingered at Mercy's bedside, checking her pulse and monitoring her saline drip. "What'll you name your new baby girl?" asked the nurse.

"Vanessa," Mercy stated matter-of-factly, then smiled at the sound of the name as it rolled off her tongue.

"Well, that's a mighty pretty name," the nurse said, smiling, and then left the room to inform T.J. of his daughter's birth.

Mercy reflected back to the day she had decided upon the name for her baby—if by chance it was to be a girl. She didn't want her to have a common name, a regular mountain name like Mercella, but a name that would propel her child into something greater in life than she herself had been able to accomplish. A name of movie stars. A name that would be unlike hers. An eloquent name that would mean something. Vanessa. A name of royalty. Just like Vanessa Redgrave.

For Mercy, it had been an uncomplicated delivery, albeit it a lengthy one: 26 hours of intense contractions and labor pains, all without any form of medication to alleviate pain. She'd had as close to a natural birth as possible, exactly the way her doctor wanted it—no medication that would potentially harm the baby.

At the youthful age of 19, she had survived. Just like all the mountain women before her, she had been strong. Just like her mother, who had survived the birth of nine children. She was pleased with herself.

By now, Mercy sensed her hospital bed being shifted at an angle. She heard the wheels unlock and shift into a forward position. Then she was rolling, rolling, rolling, toward the recovery room.

A sense of peace enveloped her weary body. Without further delay, the rocking movement calmly lulled her into restful sleep.

Hours later, she awoke in her own private room, with T.J. seated at the side of her bed. He stretched to kiss her and said, "Hey, ready for another one?"

Too tired, sore, and unwilling to accept the comment as a humorous one, Mercy scoffed, "No! Are ye crazy?!"

Ignoring her comment, he said, "I just saw her. She's beautiful, especially with all that long, black hair rolled into a tiny lil' curl on top of her head."

"Yeah, she's precious. Sure enough. Who do you think she looks like, your family or mine?" Mercy queried, silently hoping his comment would be one that would please her.

"Oh, I don't know. She looks like herself, I reckon," he said.

Indeed, she was pleased with T.J.'s response.

Vanessa will look like herself, be herself, and be unlike any other.

Following Mercy's seven-day stay in the hospital, she and T.J. prepared for their trip home to Lebanon, a trip that would force them into the worst snowstorm of the winter season.

"Well, do you think they'll let us leave with her? I mean, it's really bad out there. Just look; the snow's just pourin' down. I mean—I don't know if we *should* leave the hospital," Mercy mumbled, all the while packing a suitcase and hurriedly tucking hospital-sized baby items into her new diaper bag.

T.J. appeared to ponder her words, then said, "I don't know, but we can't stay here at the hospital. I reckon we'll just have to try and make it. I just put new chains on the tires."

Mercy had overheard WCYB's weather report earlier in the morning and learned of an increasingly fierce snowstorm headed in their direction.

How will we ever make it up Holston Mountain? And that curvy road leadin' out of Abingdon into Lebanon, with a tiny newborn?

Considering they had no alternative but to leave the safety of the hospital, Mercy and T.J. completed the necessary discharge paperwork and followed the nurse carrying their new infant. They marched outside to face February's winter wrath.

Holding the well-bundled infant in her arms, Mercy sat silently and watched as her husband cautiously maneuvered the roads leading out of Abingdon onto Highway 19. Watched as the windshield wipers groaned to keep up with the onslaught of wind and snow. Watched as they passed beyond the crest of Holston Mountain, then past Hansonville.

An inescapable sense of profound responsibility enveloped Mercy's heart and soul. An overpowering sense of accountability for the safety of her child settled in to stay forever.

As she silently prayed, she and T.J. reached the safety of their home before the full onslaught of the snowstorm.

"I'm Nobody! Who Are You?"
Emily Dickinson

I'm nobody! Who are you?
Are you nobody, too?
Then there's a pair of us — don't tell!
They'd banish us, you know.
How dreary to be somebody!
How public, like a frog
To tell your name the livelong day
To an admiring bog!

CHAPTER 43

BABY STEPS

The desire for change in one's life can be consuming, awe-inspiring. An intense, deep-felt longing to alter what may be viewed as interference with destiny. The urge to change one's fate begins a search for happiness and meaning, perhaps brought on by an innate desire to discover what may be perceived as unattainable.

Such were Mercy's dreams. Dreams that, to her, seemed at times to be as unreachable as discovering a pot of gold at the end of a rainbow.

She hadn't forgotten those dreams of attending college.

Vanessa's four years old now. I reckon if I'm aimin' to go to college, it oughta be soon. It'll be expensive. How'll I pay for it? What will T.J. think? Will he be jealous? Of course he will; isn't he always? But will he dare tell me I can't go? It won't be easy. But I'll jist have to take baby steps goin' back to school. I'll have to win him over a lil' at a time, so he can get used to the idea. He don't much like new-fangled ideas.

"Do you reckon we have enough money for me to start to school? You know, to take a night class or somethin'?" Mercy asked, all the while carefully watching T.J.'s facial expressions.

"Whaddaya wanna do that for?" he asked. "I don't know what you wanna go to that college for. What you wanna take, anyhow?"

"Oh, I don't know. Just anythin', I reckon. I gotta start somewhere—just any kinda class, it don't matter," she said.

At least now we're talkin' 'bout the possibility of me attendin' college. Baby steps. Just remember, baby steps.

As time passed, T.J. warmed to the idea, so Mercy embarked on a regimen of night classes at Southwest Virginia Community College, a new school centrally located between Richlands and Lebanon.

Although she lavished attention on Vanessa, she welcomed the change in the daily mundane routine of caring for a child. Mercy delighted in the intellectual challenges presented to her by professors at school. The conversations with other students, preparation for tests, homework assignments, and in-class debates teased her desire to further enhance her education beyond the two-year college degree.

I'll have to approach T.J. about that idea later. Just remember, baby steps. Baby steps.

During that first year, Mercy discovered she was pregnant with her second child, but refused to end her plans for furthering her education. She continued with the night classes, and T.J. cared for Vanessa. As her pregnancy progressed, she found it harder to walk the long corridors at school, drive to classes, and fit inside the desks. But she was determined; her enthusiasm would not be dampened.

At the end of the semester, Mercy gave birth to her second child.

CHAPTER 44

DEVON, ENGLAND

"What is it? What is it? Is it another lil' girl?" Mercy asked, impatiently awaiting the response from anyone willing to answer in the delivery room.

"No, it's a beautiful, healthy, baby boy," the nurse responded, all the while swaddling the newborn into a tiny blanket.

"Well, let me look at 'im. Bring 'im to me."

Mercy peered downward into the exquisite eyes of her new baby boy, those big, brown eyes so characteristic to the Musick family. And she saw her father's face.

Gently, Mercy nudged the newborn upward from her chest, then snuggled him closer to her cheek. She said. "Lord A-mercy, he looks just like R. C." She was pleased; he would look like her side of the family.

"Who's that?" a nurse responded, all the while flitting to and fro around the perimeter of the delivery room.

"Oh, that's my father. I think he looks just like 'im."

"Well, he's a beautiful baby. And a big 'un too," the nurse responded. "He weighed in at exactly eight pounds."

As she had done with her baby daughter, Mercy gently unwrapped the blanket to count the fingers and toes.

Yeah, they're all there, all right. And everythin's normal; he has ten lil' fingers and ten lil' toes.

Mercy felt the same rush of feelings she had experienced with her first born: those emotions that elicit a mother's maternal instincts, and the instantaneous bond a mother experiences with her newborn. The sense of unconditional love and the need to fiercely protect her offspring washed through her: protect him against those who might not want him, those who might harm him. "Well, what're you going to name your lil' boy?" the nurse asked.

Without hesitation, Mercy smiled and said, "Oh, we're gonna call him Devon. I already picked out the name awhile back."

"Well, isn't that a pretty name—unusual. Where'd you get that name from?"

Mercy hesitated. Reluctant to explain the reasoning or origin behind her child's name, she simply said, "Oh, we got it out of a new baby book."

But there had been much more to the name selection for her child, if by chance it was a boy. It was a name she'd seen briefly flash across the television screen, another movie star. And she'd seen the name on a map of England, too—Devon, England.

A place I'll likely never visit, she thought. To Mercy, the name sounded so mysterious and distant, somehow. Unlike common mountain names like hers, she chose to honor her son with a name of royalty. For her son, Mercy wanted a name that would propel him forward into a better life: a better life than she had been able to achieve for herself.

Keeping love of her children foremost in her mind, Mercy went through many changes in the next 20 years.

CHAPTER 45

DEATH IN
THE FAMILY

Sobs wracked Mercy's body more than once as she drove along I-20 from Augusta, GA. Trying to keep her eyes focused on heavy afternoon traffic, she glanced down at the tiny black box tucked in her lap and sobbed some more. She was mentally and physically exhausted. Today had been a longer than usual work day, and now this. Her dog, Cotton, had died earlier this morning, and she was carrying the cremated remains back home in the little box.

Two weeks before, she had left T.J. and filed for divorce. She had hired Two Men and a Truck to relocate her to a small town-house while T.J. had been at work. On that day, she had taken whatever she thought she might need, helped load heavy furniture into the moving van, and left the confines of her once-beloved home. It had been a huge undertaking, but she had made it happen—finally. She had taken her twelve-year-old dog with her, and now her precious pet was dead. It had been that type of day.

Gently lifting the black box from her car, Mercy fumbled for the keys and walked into her sparsely furnished townhouse. When leaving T.J., she had taken only basic furniture: a wrought iron picnic table for her kitchen, a wicker loveseat and chairs for the living room, their extra television, a bookshelf, and bedroom furniture. She reasoned she didn't need much, living alone.

Should I call T.J. to let him know about our dog? I haven't talked to him since I left. But he ought to know, I guess; he loved Cotton, too. Yes, I probably need to call. It seems like the right thing to do.

The phone rang and rang for almost a minute. "Hello," Mercy heard T.J.'s familiar voice.

"I just wanted to call and let you know about Cotton: she died today, and I just picked her remains up from the crematorium in Augusta."

Mercy braced herself for the verbal assault which would likely come next.

"Sorry to hear that, but you sittin' down?"

"Why do I need to sit down?"

"Well, Randy died today—your brother Randy. Been trying to get in touch with you, but didn't have your phone number."

Leaning into the phone, Mercy gasped.

Later that afternoon, she mentally compiled a list of chores she needed to complete before leaving for her brother's wake in Virginia. The following day, she refused to stay home, choosing instead the luxury of going to work. She loved her teaching job, and reasoned there was no need to drive to Virginia just yet, at least not until final arrangements could be made following an autopsy.

A sudden heart attack at the age of thirty-seven. It doesn't make sense.

Two days later, during the drive to Lebanon, Mercy glimpsed her first view of the mountains north of Spartanburg. She smiled to herself. That was always her favorite part of traveling home. Driving farther north toward Asheville, Mercy reminisced about her brother, and when she had visited with him that Christmas long ago.

"Mercy, I'm callin' from Georgia. Could I come live with you?" Randy had asked.

She remembered that phone call from Randy well. Following a second phone call, she'd agreed for her brother to come live with her and T.J., but not without hesitation and concern for how this would impact their lives. Randy was 15 years old at the time, and she'd had no contact with him since he was ten. Unfortunately, he was homeless and had nowhere else to go. It seemed he, too, had been abandoned by Nell.

Before she realized what was happening, Mercy had obtained custody of her brother, Randy. She was just 21 years old herself at the time, with a two-year-old child and in the middle of building a new house. Mercy was soon overwhelmed, with this additional responsibility in her life.

My family's always in crisis mode. Why, oh why, weren't all of us just adopted? Why weren't we placed in homes where someone actually wanted a child, and not raised at Granny and Grandpaw's, like me. And not put in a foster home, like me and Joyce. And not left to wander the streets, like Randy, or forced to leave home like Gary Wayne. There's people out there who really want children, aren't there? Where is *my mother, anyway? Why was my brother livin' on the streets? Why was he on probation? How will I raise a teenager who refuses to go back to school? Lordy, how could a mother allow her child to be homeless?!*

Over the next few months, Randy had shared with Mercy and T.J. about the hardships he'd endured while living with Nell, his experiences being homeless, and life traveling with a circus. She learned Randy had been an active participant in the circus acts, too.

"What in the world did you do in the circus, anyhow?" Mercy had asked.

With a burst of laughter, Randy said, "I stuck nails up my nose. Here, let me show you." And he did, to her amazement.

From time to time, Randy's probation officer visited to monitor his progress. For six months, Randy was seemingly content living with Mercy and T.J. But as time passed, he'd grown tired of Mercy's strict rules and boundaries: no staying out past midnight, no sneaking out of basement windows, and no smoking marijuana. Randy seemed hell-bent on breaking all the rules. Transitioning from life on the street had been hard for him.

Forced to make a decision, Mercy eventually took Randy to live with Lynn. From that point forward, her brother's life spiraled out of control. Once again without adult supervision, he had roamed the streets and continued his use of illegal drugs. Mercy was heartbroken, but knew she no longer had any influence on Randy.

Later, Randy married and had two children. He moved his family to Tennessee, then Manassas, and finally settled back in Lebanon. Life had not been easy for his family, as he continued with risky behaviors and drug use.

A tractor trailer horn blared in Mercy's ears and she was jolted back to driving. She realized she had already passed through Sam's Gap, Johnson City, and Bristol in a reckless, mind-blurring fog. Reminding herself to be more cautious, she continued her trip into Abingdon and on to Lebanon.

With tense, aching muscles, Mercy pulled into the parking lot at Combs Funeral Home. Choosing to park directly in front of the building, she steeled herself for what she knew would certainly be a stressful, uncomfortable evening. Her head throbbed but she chose to ignore it, focusing more on her dread of the family's reaction to her mother, Nell—just in case she decided to attend her son's funeral. Mercy had made certain someone in the family had contacted her mother. It was her right to know, she had argued. Every mother should know if her child dies. Leave the final decision for her mother to make—whether to attend or not.

Moving through the crowd, Mercy spoke to family members while scanning the crowd for Nell.

Surely she'd come to her own child's funeral...wouldn't she? How could she not?! Twenty years have gone by so fast since I moved from Virginia.

Choosing a seat behind the front row and directly behind her father, Mercy tried focusing on the preacher's voice but became immersed in her own thoughts. She watched the preacher's mouth move up and down repeatedly, but his words were lost on her as she turned to watch each new person enter the back doors of the chapel.

Fortunately, Mercy had missed the earlier melodrama with her father when he'd been introduced for the first time to Nell's other son: Ray's son. R.C. had a "conniption fit" right there in the break room at Combs Funeral Home.

Nell did not attend her son's funeral.

CHAPTER 46

METAMORPHOSIS

As far back as Mercy could remember, obtaining an education had been one of her top priorities in life. From that first year on Sourwood Mountain to her final year at Cleveland High School, she just knew she had to educate herself. While still married and living in Virginia, she had earned a bachelor's degree from Emory & Henry College, and had begun her teaching career at Honaker High School. After moving to South Carolina, she furthered her teaching career in Aiken County Public Schools. Mercy discovered much of her school day was spent counseling students with ADHD, bi-polar disorder, oppositional defiant disorder or other disabilities. Most cases involved students with behavior intervention plans (BIPs), and she became adept at coaching these students. She felt a connection, a compassion for these students whom others did not choose—or take the time—to understand. She was passionate about her advocacy for these students, the lost, misunderstood, and rejected ones. As a result of time spent and interest in counseling those students, Mercy pursued and obtained a master's degree in community counseling from Augusta University.

Without an advanced degree, Mercy knew her attempt to leave T.J. would have been futile. She recognized that to be successful, she had to support herself on her own, and she needed the additional income an advanced degree would provide. By now, both her children were attending college, and it was time for her to leave her loveless marriage that had gone on for way too long. She had kept her marriage together for the sake of the children; now it was time to move forward with *her* life.

With no strings attached, Mercy began her life anew following the divorce. Regrets for marrying at such a young age still haunted her, however. She would never forgive herself for making that mistake.

Never again. Never again will I lose my identity, lose myself to another man. I learned my lesson.

From the beginning, Mercy's renewed sense of freedom overwhelmed her on a daily basis. Now free to live her life without constraints, she was naïve to the new rules dictating her life as a single female. Like a toddler taking its first steps, Mercy stumbled and fell down more than once, but she stood back up and tried again. Bit by bit, she learned to navigate the strange, new world in which she now lived.

Most of all, Mercy struggled with caring for a large home, working a full-time job, and managing her finances. Frustrated with these overwhelming obligations, she found solace in additional work; any activity that kept her busy kept her emotionally centered, and sane.

Aware she needed extra income during this transitional time, Mercy took on additional responsibilities: volunteering as a counselor for abused women, teaching psychology and counseling courses at a nearby technical school, private tutoring, teaching summer school classes, and counseling alcoholics in Richmond County. Anything to provide a source of additional income.

Mercy knew that without hard work and dedication, she wouldn't survive these hard times. But her earlier experiences on Sandy Ridge Mountain, in Back Valley, in the foster home, and through 25 years of a controlling marriage had all brought her to this place in time. Hadn't she learned from her childhood? Hadn't she learned the value of hard work and perseverance? Hadn't she been raised where hard work was considered a part of everyday life? Hadn't she fed chickens, hogs and cows before going to school each morning and afternoon? Chopped and carried wood and coal? Cleaned house in her foster home until she was physically exhausted? Hadn't she completed her master's degree while working full-time, with a husband and two children? Hard work had always been part of her childhood, and it would be no different in her adult life.

With stubborn tenacity, Mercy sought out new relationships, expanded her social circle of friends, and welcomed every opportunity to expand her knowledge of counseling. In time, she learned from each negative setback she encountered. It was a period of personal growth. She would be forever thankful for those lessons she learned, albeit the hard way.

On a personal level, Mercy struggled with issues of abandonment and trust. Although she was internally aware that her concerns stemmed from the loss of her mother, as well as childhood emotional neglect, it was a consistent struggle following her divorce from T.J. At certain points, she spiraled in and out of control with emotional baggage from her past. She worked hard to stay tuned in to her conflicting emotions.

By the age of 42, Mercy's life had become a blurry fog of work, work, and more work. She became stronger with each passing year.

Four years later, in the midst of this all-consuming flurry of activity, she met Steve, a Michigan transplant who at that time lived in Florida.

Mercy remembered their first date like it was yesterday. She had agreed to meet him for dinner at Michael's Fine Dining Restaurant in Augusta, GA.

With a wide, open smile, Steve had said, "Gosh, you sound just like Flo!"

And Mercy had responded, "Well, I don't know that I like that comment. I'm just a little touchy about people making fun of my Appalachian dialect. And besides, you talk like a Yankee!"

"But I love your accent!"

Steve had redeemed himself, earning her interest from that point forward. And both were smitten from that first date.

Standing 5 feet, 6 inches tall, Steve was short—but in stature only. He had the biggest heart of any man Mercy had ever known, and this pleased her deeply. For her, he was the epitome of everything a gentleman should be—and everything T.J. could never have been. Along with a gentle, compassionate personality, Steve had an alluring, magnetic smile and a sense of humor that brought spasms of laughter and a new joy in Mercy's life. For the first time, she was introduced to how women *should* be treated: not abused, not controlled, and not demeaned. A self-made, intelligent man, Steve was secure in who he was and what he believed. Most of all, Mercy learned to trust again.

Five years after her divorce from T.J., Mercy and Steve married at the historic Partridge Inn in Augusta, joined by family and friends. Mercy had found her life partner, her soulmate. Leaving behind the remnants of her past, Mercy moved with Steve to Orlando, FL.

CHAPTER 47

ONE STEP CLOSER

It had been 36 years since Mercy had seen her mother. Through-out those years, she had never backed down from a promise she'd made to herself to find her. Every few years, she would contact her mother's twin sister in Richmond. She had called when she was in her 20s, again in her 30s, in her 40s, and now, in her 50s.

Mercy held the phone close to her ear. *Ring…ring…ring… ring.* Maybe her aunt was gone today. Maybe she'd see her number and not pick up this time.

"Hello." Mercy heard her Aunt Belle's familiar voice after several more rings.

"Hello, Aunt Belle, how're you? I was just callin' to see if you'd heard anythin' from Nell." Mercy waited for the response she already knew she'd receive. Vague answers, nothing specific enough to be able to locate her mother.

"Well…Mercy, how're you? Honey, your mother's doin' fine. I talked to her jist yesterday. She's havin' some more problems with her stomach, though. How're you doin'?"

Mercy recognized her Aunt's attempt to change the subject.

Keep the conversation focused and pull the subject back to Nell.

Mercy said "I'm doin' fine. What's wrong with Mother's stomach?"

"Well, you know she ain't been right after that colon cancer. She's got a stomach hernia."

Without hesitation, Mercy blurted out, "Well, what caused that, you reckon?"

"Well, I think it has somethin' to do with that surgery she had to remove the cancer. Don't know for sure, and Nell ain't sure herself."

They chatted about run-of-the-mill things, but Mercy shifted the subject back to Nell. Having lost patience, she was determined to be more aggressive with her aunt this time. "Well, you know, I'm living in Orlando now. I already know Mother's in Perry, Florida, so I wanted to find her specific address," she rambled, but still attempted to stay on track.

A pause on the other end of the line. "Well, you know I can't tell you where she is, Mercy. She made me promise years ago not to tell nobody where she was. I'm her sister, and I love her; I talk to her about every day to stay in touch, but…"

"Well, I want to know where she is."

"Honey, I'd love to tell you, but she said not to."

Mercy felt her blood pressure boil over from frustration. "Aunt Belle, if my mother dies, I want to be notified! And I expect you to let me know when that happens!"

Another pause. "Well, let me talk to Tabatha about it and see what she says."

What the hell?! A half-sister I've never seen or talked to before has to be consulted about whether I can visit my mother, or be notified of her death?! Lordy, I need a margarita, maybe two... or maybe three.

As expected, Aunt Belle had refused to provide any helpful information. Infuriated by her aunt's unwillingness to share a phone number or address, Mercy determined she would find her mother on her own, without assistance from anyone else.

How ironic: I'm living in Florida somewhere near my mother. All the way from Sandy Ridge in Southwest Virginia, and we both live in Florida. Surely it's destiny. Well, I won't be outdone this time!

Exhaustive internet searches provided some contact information, so Mercy placed endless phone calls to each Ninella Head she found online. Her time on the phone resulted in not one single clue to her mother's existence—just some embarrassing conversations with strangers. At least she knew the name of the town: Perry, FL.

The following day, Mercy dialed the phone number for the county clerk's office in Taylor County, FL. Mustering up her most efficient, pleasant voice, she said, "Yes Ma'am, I'm trying to locate my birth mother, Esta Ninella Head. I believe she lives in your town. Do you have any records on file for her?"

"Honey, that's an unusual name. Did you say Esta Ninella Head? Could you spell that for me, please?"

Mercy did. She heard the *clickety click click* of the computer keys.

"No, Ma'am; there's nothing in the system. Could it be under another name?"

"Well, maybe. Her last known married name was Esta Brown."

"Let me check." Again, *clickety click click.*

Mercy held her breath and waited…and waited some more.

"Yes, Ma'am, there is an Esta Brown."

"Could I have a copy of any records that may be on file for her, please?"

"You'll have to mail a request and pay a fee, but they're public records," the clerk said.

Of course I will. I've located my mother! Surely a phone number and address would be on court records.

For days, Mercy waited to receive the documents in the mail. One week later, she nervously ripped into the yellow envelope from Taylor County, FL. A post office address and a phone number were all she found—no physical home address. Mercy was disappointed, but not ready to give in to defeat.

Later that afternoon, Mercy sat sipping iced tea on the back lanai of her Florida home. Her mind wandered as she stared across the manicured lawn at the palm trees surrounding her sparkling pool. A wide array of tropical plants and flowers gave Mercy privacy from her neighbors. The bird-of-paradise tree, Hawaiian ti, shrimp plants, Heliconiaceae plant species, African violets, and smaller decorative palms provided a sense of living in the tropics. The repetitious soothing sound of the hot tub waterfall mesmerized her, causing her eyes to droop toward sleep. She needed a little shut-eye.

The doorbell rang several times with barely a pause between. Roused from slumber, Mercy walked groggily past the sliding doors and through the living room, then peeped through the sidelights. It was her friend, Michelle; Mercy had been expecting her.

"Hey, Michelle. I just had you on my mind, girl. Come on in!"

With a huge smile on her face, Michelle joined Mercy on the

back lanai. "You've been thinking about me? What's up?" Michelle queried with perfect articulation.

An English teacher at Timber Creek High School, Michelle had perfect poise and diction, always carefully pronouncing every syllable. Mercy admired that since she herself had never learned to speak that way. She could code-switch her dialect, if necessary. But she didn't like doing it; she enjoyed being herself.

"Well, I've got a huge favor to ask of you," Mercy said.

"You know I would do whatever I could for my best bud. What's the favor?"

Mercy hesitated. She knew it was an unusual request, but she was committed to doing whatever was necessary to locate her mother. "You know my whole story about trying to find my mother, right? Well, I received the paperwork from her county in the mail today, but it didn't include an address. I need you to call this phone number and pretend you're from the Social Security Office."

Michelle's blue eyes sparkled. She knew the entire story about Mercy, but pretending to be a Social Security representative could be construed as some form of criminal activity. "Well, why can't *you* call?"

"She might recognize my voice, or at least become suspicious because of my dialect. You don't talk like me, you know."

I can't talk to my mother, at least not yet. Not just yet. I need more time before speaking with her. I'll talk to her in person soon—very soon.

Pondering the idea for a brief moment, Michelle said, "Let's do it. Where's your phone?"

Comfortable with her decision, Michelle dialed Nell's phone number and started talking. "Yes, Ma'am, I'm from the Social Security Office. We're attempting to update our contact information. Our records indicate you're receiving your Social Security checks each month at the following address: P.O. Box nine twenty-one, Perry, Florida. Is that correct?"

"Why, yes, Honey, that's right," stated the pleasant voice at the other end of the line.

"Well, we need your exact *physical* address, the location of your home. What is that, Ma'am?"

Michelle quickly jotted it down. "Okay, Ma'am. Thank you, and have a good day."

The ruse had worked.

That afternoon, as soon as Steve walked through the door and joined Mercy on the lanai, she blurted out, "Steve, we're going to Perry, Florida on Friday. Michelle and I located my mother today. With one simple phone call."

"What do you mean *we're* going to Perry, Florida? Not me," he quipped.

"Yes, *you*. I want you to be there with me. I need your support doing this. I've waited all these years to find her, and I need you," said Mercy, her big brown Musick eyes pleading.

"But why? I don't know what to say or do. How did all this happen, anyway?"

As quickly as possible, Mercy explained the details of the day's events.

Sensing he was already defeated, Steve backed down and reluctantly agreed to accompany his wife to Perry. He knew how much this meant to his new wife. She had spent years attempting to locate her mother. He couldn't, he wouldn't, refuse her this request.

CHAPTER 48

NELL IS FOUND

Two days later, Mercy drove cautiously past her mother's rural home. She surveyed the expansive front lawn of sparse Floratam grass intertwined with native weeds, pine trees, and a multitude of Florida undergrowth. She was careful not to speed past the dirt driveway, slowing the car long enough to verify the address painted on the unassuming mailbox. A wooden black and white milk cow stared back at her, its permanent stance clearly out of place with the surrounding thicket of Florida palmettos.

Do I have the fortitude to confront my mother after all these years? Can I use my best counseling skills in a non-confrontational way, in an attempt to find the answers I need? Can I remember to ask open-ended questions? Will I find closure? How do I respond if my mother refuses to acknowledge me as her daughter?

Who's living with my mother now, and how will they react to my visit? Do they even know *my mother abandoned her children? Is this a dangerous situation I've placed myself in at this point? Should I invite my husband to accompany me inside, or would he be safer remaining outside while I initiate the first contact?*

There were a multitude of unanswered questions with so many concerns and so many fears.

After checking into a local motel, Mercy and Steve drove to the largest store in town: Walmart. They needed a plan of action, another ruse. The timing was perfect, they decided. Tomorrow was Mother's Day, and flowers would be an appropriate peace offering to her mother. After searching through the entire store, Mercy finally chose the largest peace lily from among the selection of flowers.

By then, it was midafternoon. Loading the oversized plant into the car, Mercy and Steve retraced the drive back to Nell's and drove straight into the long, sandy driveway.

Now is the time; there's no backing out now. Things will work out. If they don't, I'll be no worse off. I have *to see my mother.*

Loosening her seatbelt and stepping from the car, Mercy moved without further hesitation toward her mother's trailer, carrying her peace offering. Knocking timidly with her left hand on the front door, Mercy balanced the heavy plant on her hip with her other arm, stepping backward as the storm door creaked outward in her direction.

"Yes, can I help you?" the elderly man asked. No pause or concern at opening the door to a stranger, Mercy noticed.

"Yes, I have a floral delivery for Esta Brown. Does she live here?" Mercy asked. She took note of his fragile features and unsteady gait, and determined he was of no physical threat to her. At least not yet, she thought. She was still uncertain as to the predicament she'd gotten herself into.

"Why yeah, she's here. Just a minute, I'll get her for you." He turned away from Mercy, leaving the door ajar, providing her with the opportunity to peek inside her mother's living room. Squinting into the darkened room, Mercy watched as the elderly man disappeared around the corner into the back of the home.

Feeling her heartbeat accelerate, Mercy struggled to breathe. She felt a flush creep up her neck, moving hotly past her mouth, nose, and forehead as it consumed her face. Now was the moment. Now was the time for her to meet her mother, Nell.

Steadying herself and attempting to maintain her hold on the oversized peace lily with one hand, Mercy watched as Nell rounded the corner and moved toward her. This was the moment Mercy had envisioned for so many years; she wanted to memorize every single feature, every crevice in her mother's aged face, and smell the aroma from her mother's skin for the first time in such a long time. Just like a new baby, Mercy felt she was being born again.

Attempting to continue her plan to disguise herself and the true purpose for being there, Mercy asked, "Hi, are you Esta Brown?"

"Why, yes, I am, Honey," Nell said.

"Well, I'm delivering flowers for you today from Perry's Florist Shop in town. Here they are. Aren't they pretty?" Mercy pasted a friendly smile on her face and shoved the peace lily toward her mother.

Taking further note of her mother's small frame and aging body, Mercy reconsidered. She said, "Are you sure you can carry them? They're pretty heavy. Here, let me put them on the table for you." She turned toward the closest small table, near the front door, and gently placed them beside an oversized chair.

Mercy was uncertain if Perry's Florist Shop even existed, but she assumed every small town had at least one florist. She was committed to moving forward with her ruse, determined to engage her mother in conversation.

One step at a time. Just move with the natural flow of things. And breathe.

With a confused expression, Nell said, "Well, who in the world would've sent these?"

Hastily removing the card which had been carefully tucked inside the plant, Mercy handed it to her mother. She observed the slight shaking in her own hand.

Nell read the card aloud. "Happy Mother's Day. With love, from your daughter."

"Well, ain't that strange. I been with Tabatha all day long, and she didn't say one word about getting' me any flowers. But that ain't like her to buy me flowers no how." Mercy had already known about her half-sister, Tabatha. Years before, she'd shed countless tears when this sister was born, the one who had replaced *her* in her mother's life.

It's only natural for her to think they're from Tabatha. But the comment stung Mercy's heart and left a bitter, acidic taste in her mouth.

"Well, that was really sweet of her to send you flowers. You know tomorrow is Mother's Day. By the way, you really do have a nice place here, Ms. Brown. I've never been out in this section of Perry." Mercy rattled off whatever innocuous comments came to mind, attempting to continue any type of conversation.

"Yeah, we like it here. It's peaceful; ain't nobody to bother you out here in the country," Nell commented, oblivious to Mercy's purpose or her identity.

Mercy hoped to continue the conversation as she sauntered toward the oversized chair in the living room. By now, she felt the exhaustion caused by her three-hour drive from Orlando and the trip to pick out the flower; she needed to rest. She suspected that if she seated herself comfortably in a nearby chair, she could engage her mother in further dialogue. But she reminded herself not to be too presumptuous.

"Phew, it's been a long day. Do you mind if I sit down and chat for a while, Ms. Brown?"

"Why no, not at all, Honey. Have a seat."

Mercy removed her glasses. In a last-minute attempt to disguise her face, she had covered her eyes with oversized sunglasses, suspecting her mother would immediately recognize her large brown Musick eyes and refuse to speak with her.

"How long you lived here, Ms. Brown?"

"Aw, 'bout twenty-five years now, I reckon."

Mercy probed even further, "Is that your husband I met at the door?"

"Naw, he ain't my husband. We ain't married. He's just a friend," Nell responded, obviously comfortable with her response and with no hint of embarrassment or need for further explanation as to why she was living with a man, but unmarried.

"What's your friend's name?"

"He's Jim."

Mercy sensed she was moving too quickly into her mother's personal territory and grew uncomfortable with her own line of questioning.

It was a surreal moment in time. Like an actor who had rehearsed her lines over and over only to suffer intense stage fright on opening night, Mercy now lost all memory of those well-practiced lines. Almost feeling like she was having an out-of-body experience, Mercy wafted between what was reality and the role she was playing.

Determined it was the appropriate time to end her ruse, Mercy said, "You don't know me, do you?"

Straightening up her shoulders and leaning forward from her position on the sofa, Nell said, "Well, no... No, I don't. Who are ye?" Lines in her face creased and Mercy detected a sense of irritation in her mother's voice, with just the slightest twinge of hoarseness. Mercy remembered that voice so well from the past.

"I'm Mercy." Still no visible reaction from her mother, even after hearing the name.

"Mercy. Mercy who?" Nell frowned.

Staring directly into her mother's eyes, Mercy said, "I'm your daughter, Mercy."

Keeping eye contact, Mercy moved from the chair and dropped to her knees on the floor at her mother's feet. She stammered, "I forgive you, Mother."

There was no mention of *why* she was forgiving her, no explanation.

With an appalled, open-mouthed expression, Nell lifted her hands to shield her face—and wept. Mercy watched her mother cry, allowing her time to process the revelation. Then Mercy moved upward to wrap her arms around her mother. They embraced, kissed one another's cheeks, and then leaned outward to search one another's eyes and savor the tender moment.

CHAPTER 49

MERCY LEARNS MORE ABOUT NELL

Within the hour, Mercy was introduced to her half-sister Tabatha, who was even more surprised to meet her.

"Oh, this is the best Mother's Day present you could've ever given Mama," Tabatha cooed, then cried as she embraced her half-sister for the first time.

All this while, Steve had been passing time in the car with the engine idling, waiting for any sign from Mercy. It was their plan to keep the car ready for any response, in the event Mercy was unwelcome in the home. Realizing Steve was likely concerned by now, Mercy opened the front storm door, waved a thumbs-up, and waited to introduce him to her mother.

Shutting off the engine, Steve got out of the car and sauntered toward the front door. His expression pleaded for an explanation from Mercy. But she had none, just a smile.

Nell yelled, "Well, come on in here. We ain't gonna bite ye." Then she added, "Come on in here and lemme take a good look at ye."

Reluctantly stepping into the living room, Steve looked toward Mercy for reassurance, then extended his hand toward Nell.

"Hello, I'm Steve, Mercy's husband. It's a pleasure to finally meet you."

"Well, I'm glad to meet you, Steve. Mercy says you're a purty special person. I reckon you must be, to marry one of them Musicks," Nell said.

Steve laughed but made no comment.

"Hey, Jim, come in here," Nell yelled in her loud, raspy voice.

Taking advantage of the lapse in conversation, Mercy glanced around the room, searching the walls and shelves for any photos of her, Darrell, Gary Wayne, Joyce, Lynn, or Randy. As she surveyed the living room, she took note of a number of framed pictures. None of the faces peering back at her looked familiar. There were no visible indications that Nell had ever had a previous family.

Mercy felt the first pangs of disappointment. Here was proof that she and her siblings had not been remembered: their existence not even acknowledged by one single photo.

As Jim's aged body slowly rounded the corner, he stepped into the living room, a quizzical expression on his face. He appeared confused about these new visitors, as well as Nell's serious expression.

Nell quipped, "Jim, I want you to meet my daughter, my daughter, Mercy." Then she paused to monitor his reaction.

With his mouth gaping wide, Jim stood quietly and stared closely into Nell's face, then glanced toward Mercy. "*What*? This is your *daughter*?"

"You heard me. Yeah, this is my daughter Mercy," Nell responded without a hint of trepidation.

Jim moved toward Mercy and clasped her hand. "It's nice to meet you, Mercy." That was it: no probing questions for Nell. Mercy wondered if he would later interrogate her mother.

It was an awkward meeting as each person took turns exchanging pleasantries about the weather and the trip from Orlando, and asking carefully-guarded questions about other family members. By mid-afternoon, the conversation turned to eating dinner; everyone was hungry. By this time, Tabatha's husband and children had joined the family group, along with Nell's sixteen-year-old granddaughter—the one Nell and Jim were now raising in their home.

So...my mother gave up her own children, to later have three more children, then raise a granddaughter. That doesn't make any sense to me. None at all.

Inquiring about food and directions to the nearest restaurant, Steve rushed to Perry for a drive-thru order of Chinese food. Piles of General Tao's chicken, egg foo yung, fried rice, and egg rolls were shuffled to the backyard picnic table, giving the family ample space to enjoy their afternoon meal in a more relaxed atmosphere. All the while, Mercy swatted gnats and tried to ignore Florida's sweltering heat.

Over the dinner table, Mercy and her mother reminisced about living on Sandy Ridge in the mountains of Southwest Virginia. Tabatha and her husband speculated about how it might be to live high up on a mountain, how they could hunt, and fish in the mountain streams. Both were avid outdoorsmen, and were mesmerized by Mercy's stories about her mountains. They shared their love of hunting wild boars, shooting deer, fishing in the local rivers, and riding four wheelers deep into Florida's dense undergrowth. Tabatha's three children listened but added little to the conversation, choosing to simply absorb the new information, then move on to their favorite pastime— just being teenagers. Mercy noted that Jim, too, had little to say during the meal.

He's probably not even aware of my mother's entire background, at least not the full details. Neither is Tabatha.

Later in the night, Mercy and Steve left for their hotel, promising a brief visit the next day before returning to Orlando. Overall, Mercy thought her long-awaited visit with her birth mother had been a pleasant one.

The following day was a short visit—just to say goodbyes, exchange phone numbers, and addresses—with another promise for Mercy, Tabatha, and Nell to stay in contact with one another.

For the next few months, Mercy found every opportunity to call her mother, enjoying the newfound mother-daughter relationship. She hung on to every story Nell shared with her: stories about her birth, stories about hardships and surviving in Back Valley and Sandy Ridge, stories about R.C.'s physical abuse, and tales of Nell's experiences since leaving the mountains of Virginia.

However, during one phone conversation, Nell quipped, "What're you doin' calling so much! You know I hate talkin' on the phone."

Mercy was confused and temporarily stunned by her mother's

unexpected comment. Stammering, Mercy replied, "I don't know. I guess I just wanted to talk to my mother." She made a mental note not to call her mother so often in the future.

"Well, I jist hate talkin' on a damn phone. Everybody knows that by now. My sister calls me ever day, and I jist hate it. Sometimes I don't even wanna answer the dad-blasted thing!"

My mother sure is a cold woman. After all these years of not talkin' to me, she wants me to call less. Strange woman. She's a proud, stubborn, private woman, too. And what about those emotional swings?

Mercy called her mother less on the telephone after that, but when they did talk, Nell regularly spoke about her twin sister Belle, who lived in Richmond, VA.

"I'd sure like to see my twin sister jist one more time before I die," she'd say. And then move just as quickly in another direction, relating yet another unknown story to Mercy. As the weeks passed, it was increasingly difficult and unnerving for Mercy as she tried to predict her mother's mood swings from one telephone call to another.

Recalling her mother's stories about an earlier bout with colon cancer and her obviously declining health, Mercy considered her mother's wish to see her twin. More than anything, she wanted to please her mother. Since she hoped to develop a closer relationship, a surprise trip to Richmond seemed a minimal way to accomplish that feat. Mercy discussed it with Steve and they both agreed it would be a gracious gift to take her mother to see her beloved twin sister in person, one more time.

During their next phone conversation, Mercy asked, "Mother, would you like to fly to Richmond to see your twin sister? Don't worry; I'll pay all the expenses involved. You'd just need to pack. I'll come and pick you up in Perry, and then we'll fly out of Orlando."

With some hesitation at leaving Jim and her granddaughter at home alone, Nell finally agreed to a week-long trip to Richmond and a visit back to Sandy Ridge Mountain. Excited beyond words, Mercy looked forward to spending quality time with her mother.

And so the trip to Richmond, VA was planned, a special trip with mother and daughter traveling alone. Mercy had no inkling of how this trip would change her expectations for her mother, Nell.

CHAPTER 50

FULL CIRCLE

Mercy traveled along the Highway 417 toll road, shifted to the 528 Beeline Expressway, and exited onto Semoran Boulevard, leading to Orlando International Airport. As expected, the city of Orlando and the airport sweltered in the August heat on this day. Not a single ocean breeze stirred the Queen Palms lining the main entrance to the airport. Cascading along the well-manicured entranceway, pampas grass, sago palms, oleander bushes, and Hawaiian ti plants stood wilting in the blistering heat, their leaves drooping in the afternoon sun. Mercy detested the thought of battling Florida's smothering, summer heat, but she reminded herself how excited she was about this first mother-daughter trip. After a short delay at Orlando International Airport, mother and daughter boarded the plane headed from Orlando to Richmond.

Without incident, Mercy and Nell arrived at Aunt Belle's home: a tiny, neat structure tucked among the newer sprawling subdivisions in the city. Surrounded by a small, well-tended lawn, the home was cozy and unpretentious, making it stand out from the newly built houses. It was a reminder of older generations and inhabitants of the city's past.

Belle graciously offered Mercy and Nell the upstairs guest bedroom. A cozy room with low-slanted ceilings, it held two mismatched beds topped with quaint, homemade quilts and two bedside lamps on small, simple tables. It's more than comfortable, Mercy thought. Following a late afternoon meal, Mercy and Nell retired for the night, chatting, laughing, and sharing more untold stories late into the night. Mercy could not have been happier.

The following morning, Mercy made a mental note to pay for whatever supplies she and her mother might need for their visit with Aunt Belle. She planned a trip to the closest grocery store. Remembering her mother's proud, private ways, Mercy considered how she could pay for all the items without offending her mother.

After a light breakfast, they all loaded into Aunt Belle's oversized van, chatting and laughing all the way to Gene's Supermarket. While inside the store, Mercy traipsed up and down the aisles, reminding herself to follow at a distance and not to hover over her mother. She had noticed how Nell sometimes grew defensive if Mercy lingered too close or offered to pay for anything.

Turning around in the aisle, Nell noticed Mercy tagging along behind her. "Why don't you find something else to do while I'm in here?" Nell warned, with an unmistakable, chastising tone in her voice.

Mercy moved to the far end of the store, giving her mother the personal space she likely needed. Up and down the aisles she shopped, selecting items for lunch, dinner, and afternoon snacks.

In a short time, Mercy had chosen her items, placing them neatly into her grocery cart, and completed her check-out quickly. But Nell was nowhere to be found; Mercy became concerned about her mother. She'd hoped to pay for her mother's groceries. Lugging her paper bags, Mercy roamed through the fresh vegetable section, meandered around the dairy department, and continued searching for her mother. With no good fortune in her search, Mercy left the store. Scanning the main entrance, she lingered outside for a moment, then returned to search along the aisles for her mother again. Finally, Mercy returned to Aunt Belle's van.

And there sat Nell and Aunt Belle.

Without the slightest delay, Nell yelled, "What'd you go back in that damned store lookin' for me for?" She glared at Mercy much like Granny used to.

Like a reprimanded child, Mercy's eyes lowered as she evaded her mother's angry stare. She tried to ignore the biting, hurtful, unwarranted words spewed by her mother, and she was at a loss to verbalize her feelings. What had she done wrong? Why was her mother upset with her? Tears stung Mercy's eyes, but she refused to allow them to flow; she refused to show any outward signs of hurt feelings.

Mercy timidly responded, "I don't know, Mother; I was just worried about you."

"Well, ye don't need to worry 'bout me. I can take care of myself!"

Aunt Belle sat silently. She knew her sister's personality well enough, and thought it best not to involve herself in the uncomfortable conversation. She simply started the engine, backed out of the parking spot, and pulled onto the highway leading back to her house on Miami Avenue.

During the return trip, tension escalated between Nell and

Mercy. Struggling to restrain her tears, Mercy leaned her body toward the door, away from her mother's view from the backseat, and wiped her tears each time they threatened to overflow.

Mother won't see me crying. Not ever! Never. I'm not a child; I'm not that five-year-old little girl she abandoned. I won't cry! I won't.

It was a pivotal moment of clarity for Mercy. Her mother would never be the type of mother she had hoped for and needed. Her search had been about a fantasy: finding a loving, nurturing mother who would make every attempt to rectify the mistakes she had made abandoning her, a mother who would willingly display contrition and repentance. The first seeds of regret planted themselves in Mercy's mind.

Back at Aunt Belle's, Mercy cautioned herself about further angering her mother. Still confused and questioning what she had done to make her mother so angry, Mercy kept her distance. But she couldn't deliberately ignore her mother, at least not for seven days, she thought. Hoping the fresh, outside air would clear her thoughts, Mercy stepped out the front door, crossed the yard, and flopped into a chair that Aunt Belle had placed under a large canopy. It was a comfortable, shaded area meant for relaxing, and Mercy was thankful for just such a spot; she needed time to sort out her emotions, and determine how to clear the air between mother and daughter.

As she turned in the lawn chair, Mercy spotted her mother seated on a bench backed up against the front door. She had walked right by her mother without realizing it. But it was too late; she had to face her mother now.

Nell said, "You might as well go on back in *that* house now. Just leave me alone, just leave me by myself!"

And Mercy did just that, quietly retreating to the upstairs bedroom, wounded beyond repair by her mother's hateful words.

How dare she! I've searched for my mother for 36 years, and now she wants me to leave her alone! What the hell?! Haven't I left her alone long enough?

Reacting to her mother's hurtful, biting comments, Mercy wept violent tears. Stretched out prone on the bed, she wept into the faded, cotton lace pillows, trying to stifle her sobs. For at least a half hour, she chastised herself for her knee-jerk reactions, and eventually questioned whether she might be overreacting. Hadn't she always prided herself on being tough, not shedding tears in front of co-workers and bosses, and keeping control as a professional female? But in her personal life, it was a different story.

Mercy reprimanded herself for being in her current position: all alone in Richmond. She needed Steve; she ached for his presence. Mercy needed his loving arms to envelop her, wanted him to touch her face and promise her everything would be better tomorrow. Steve could always comfort her as no other person in her entire life had been able to.

Dabbing at her eyes, Mercy slowly rose from the bed and straightened out her wrinkled clothes. After a few deep breaths to settle herself, she carefully remade the bed and began repacking her suitcase, stuffing items inside without much thought.

Oh, why didn't I beg Steve to come with me? I can't stay in Richmond for this entire vacation with my mother. Not for seven days! I'm fifty-six years old. I refuse to be treated like a child. I'm so disappointed in how I've reacted to all this. I'll find a way, some way, to leave this place tonight. I suspect my mother is sick, maybe even suffers from a bi-polar disorder. Or worse, and that scares me. I can't deal with all that. I can't spend another minute with my irrational, cold-hearted mother.

Without a word to anyone, Mercy carefully plotted her escape from Aunt Belle's home. She needed to remove herself from her mother's angry stares and the stress of dealing with Nell's meltdown. By late afternoon, she would find someone, anyone, to drive her to the nearest hotel or airport. She did, a family member she'd never known, someone she felt would be discreet and allow her to leave without probing questions.

Rolling the suitcase down the stairs with the least amount of noise possible, Mercy halted at the bottom of the steps. Now was the moment for her escape.

Alerted by the sounds, everyone paused their conversations and glanced in her direction as she entered the living room. Mercy knew there would be no leaving without some form of explanation.

In the most pleasant, cordial voice she could summon, Mercy said, "Hey, I thought I'd go to a hotel for the night."

Nell glared at her from across the room. No comment. Just awkward silence.

Aunt Belle insisted, "Oh, no, you've got to stay. We've got plenty of room here; you don't need to go to a hotel."

"No, I've decided to go. I'm already packed," Mercy said.

Still no comment from Nell. Just that cold stare.

Shifting the suitcase toward the front door, Mercy smiled, then calmly walked across the room and hugged her Aunt Belle. She then attempted to kiss her mother. At the last moment, Nell turned her cheek away.

"Y'all enjoy the rest of your vacation. I love you."

No response from Nell. Nothing.

As Mercy walked through the front door and onto the lawn, she knew this would be the last time she'd ever see her mother. She recalled when she was five years old and had sobbed for her mother the day she'd been abandoned. She also remembered the painful times she'd sought her mother's arms, searched for her in Bluefield as she traveled with Uncle Lawrence on her trip to Narrows, and struggled all these years to find her.

Life is not always fair. Be careful what you ask for.

Later in the hotel room, Mercy reminisced about the tender moment when she'd first found her mother, how they'd hugged and how Nell had cried. She knew her mother loved her, in her own way. It had been a special moment between mother and daughter. She was thankful for that moment. Remembering their conversations the night before, Mercy reflected on how they'd spent much-needed quality time sharing stories and laughing late into the night. She was thankful for that one special night. She knew those memories would have to be enough.

Throughout that long night at the hotel, Mercy was a bundle of nerves, tossing, turning, and fidgeting in her sleep. When morning finally arrived, it signaled a brighter day for her; she had cleared her mind and was resolute in what she needed to do. That morning, she flew home to Orlando and the loving arms of her husband.

Clearly, she'd made a huge mistake in the quest to locate her mother. She'd come full circle in her life. After her divorce from T.J., she'd promised herself she would no longer suffer *any* form of abuse or attempts at being controlled, and she would remove herself from those who would cause her emotional pain.

Relying on her training as a counselor, she realized there could be no meaningful future with her mother. She must disengage, remove herself from someone who was cold, embittered and emotionally harmful to her. Mercy must take care of her own well-being.

And so, Mercy abandoned Nell.

AFTERTHOUGHT

Seven years later, Nell died in a nursing home near Perry, FL. According to her daughter Tabatha, Nell had requested to be cremated, and for her ashes to be scattered on the family cemetery on Sandy Ridge Mountain. The following obituary was placed in the town's newspaper:

Esta Ninella Brown, 83, passed away on July 13, 2016 in Perry, FL. Esta was born March 17, 1933 in Wilder, Virginia, to Charles Edgar Head and Josie Bell Sutherland Head. She enjoyed spending time with her grandchildren and gardening. Esta was preceded in death by her longtime companion of 32 years. She is survived by one sister and her daughter, Tabatha.

LIFE LESSONS

1. **<u>Don't believe what they *say*...believe what they *do*. Ignore the words, just watch your husband's actions. They're clues.</u>** So if he says he loves you and then slaps you up b'side the head...*run*.

2. **<u>If you're desperate to be loved and co-dependent, recognize it.</u>** "I love you, Bitch," ain't the way a man oughta talk to his wife. Bein' called a bitch ain't nice...*run*.

3. **<u>Physical abuse is unacceptable.</u>** If he hits you and your eyes are all black n' blue, don't lie for him...don't walk away...*run*.

4. **<u>Intimidation is demeaning and damaging to one's self-esteem.</u>** If he threatens to divorce you if you don't vote for a

Democrat...*run*...but first, go and vote for that Republican!

5. **<u>Ridicule is another form of abuse.</u>** If he makes fun of you and belittles your family, even if your family is Manson-like, they're *your* family...*run.*

6. **<u>Verbal abuse is unacceptable.</u>** If he calls you a *%@# bitch every day...don't walk...*run.*

7. **<u>Possessive jealousy is a form of control.</u>** If he tells you he loves you way too early, questions every man you speak to on the street, and is jealous of every man who ever courted you...or even *thought* about courtin' you...*run.*

8. **<u>Believe the threats.</u>** If he makes a threat and tells you to shut up or he'll shut you up, he means it. Don't walk...*run.*

9. **<u>Problems controlling anger are real.</u>** When you see that balled-up fist comin' straight for your head, you'd better duck...then *run.*

10. **<u>Insecurity breeds contempt, abuse, and controlling behaviors.</u>** If you've done everythin' in your power to make your man feel good in the marriage, but you can't, it's outa your hands...*run.*

11. **<u>Being called "The Old Lady" is not endearing.</u>** Let's face it. No woman *really* wants to be called "The Old Lady." It ain't cute...*run.*

12. **<u>Listen to your inner feelings.</u>** Let's be honest here. If you

get to the point where you dread comin' through that front door and seein' his face...*run*.

13. **<u>Stifling another person's independence is a control issue.</u>** If you want to go out and socialize with your friends, do it. If he don't like it...*run*.

14. **<u>Lying about abuse enables the abuser.</u>** If you lie about him hittin' you, you're keepin' a harmful family secret. Don't do it...*run*.

15. **<u>Do not stay in an abusive marriage for the sake of the children.</u>** Don't stay in the home for the young'uns. They know what's goin' on. Don't stay, don't pretend this is normal, don't allow this to continue to the next generation...*run*.

16. **<u>Seek counseling at the earliest signs of dysfunction</u>**. If you want counselin' for your husband, that's fine...just know it's unlikely to last...*run*.

17. **<u>Controlling someone is not love.</u>** If you feel like you've been loved to death, you probably have been...*run*.

18. **<u>Do not argue and fight in front of children.</u>** If you do, it ain't right. Jist get them young'uns and...*run*.

19. **<u>The best predictor of future behavior is *past* behavior.</u>** If that balled-up fist hits you in the right eye, that balled-up fist will later hit you *twice* in the left eye; it gets worse, not better over time...*run*.

20. **Recognize the cyclical honeymoon phases of abuse; things get better, but that will not last long at all.** If he buys you flowers and swears, "I'll never do it again," don't you dare believe 'im. It'll happen again, and worse...*run*.

21. *Stay* **away. Do not return to the abusive environment.** Don't go anywhere with him "jist to talk." He don't want to talk; he wants to tell you lies and beat your ass...*run*.

22. **When he blames you for his feelings and actions, this is manipulation.** *He* **is responsible for his feelings and actions.** If he says "You make me mad," or "You're the reason I get so mad," that's crazy talk. It ain't *your* fault...*run*.

23. **When he attempts to isolate you, this is manipulation and control.** If he tries to keep you from visitin' your kinfolk and neighbors...*run*.

24. **When he uses different kinds of force during arguments, he is becoming more violent.** If he kicks, pulls your hair, shoves, grabs your clothes, slaps you, or punches your head...*run*.

25. **Threatening to take your children away or refusing to allow you to take them is manipulation and control.** Catch that asshole asleep, then take them young'uns and...*run*.

26. **Statements like "No one else would ever have you. You're lucky to have me!" are meant to demean and control.** You know this ain't true...*run*.

27. <u>**Rigidly controlling finances is an attempt to maintain your dependence upon him, to keep you a victim. You need to be financially independent.**</u> Hide a lil' money in a cannin' jar, and bury it where he can't find it. If you have time, dig up that jar and...*run.*

28. <u>**Refusal to accept anger management is a problem. This is denial.**</u> He'll have a hard time with this one. You know he has a problem, your whole Manson-like family knows he has a problem, his family knows he has a problem, all your friends know he has a problem—but he won't never own up to it...*run.*

29. <u>**An abuse victim's most vulnerable time is when she attempts to leave. The abuser is most likely to seriously injure or *kill* a spouse when they are leaving the home.**</u> If you decide to leave, do it fast! Don't be greedy, neither. You don't need that nice kitchen table n' chairs nearly as much as you need to be alive. You can eat off that picnic table...*run.*

A READER'S GUIDE

1. *In Search of Nell* is written in third-person omniscient narrative. Why does the author frame the novel in this manner? How effective would the book have been if written in first-person narrative? What might have been missed or altered if it had been written in first person?

2. How does the author discuss and explore class differences in the novel? Think about Mercy's friends, coal miners, city vs. small town folk, city vs. rural, rich vs. poor.

3. In the beginning of the novel, how does the author depict Mercy? Why does Mercy love Sandy Ridge Mountain so much? Why does she learn to love Back Valley?

4. How is Mercy's life depicted after she moves away from

Back Valley? How does Mercy change as she grows older? How does the narrator note the change? Explain how Mercy's internal dialogue is altered as she grows older.

5. What is the significance of the chapter "I-N-G" to Mercy, and perhaps other people in Appalachia? Is the Appalachian dialect an effective method for characterizing the people in the novel? What Appalachian words were used in the book? What specific traditional Appalachian customs are mentioned?

6. What do Granny's rules tell you about her character? Do you think these are typical or atypical of her beliefs as a Baptist?

7. Why did Mercy marry at such a young age? How/when does Mercy recognize she made a mistake to marry so early in life? How does Mercy change after marriage? Why do you think the author skips 20 years in the novel, picking up the story after the divorce? What clues indicate the purpose for this jump in time?

8. What is the significance of the chapter "Play Purties?" How does leaving Teddy impact Mercy? Why was Teddy so coveted?

9. What did Mercy learn from her experiences in so many different homes? Were they positive or negative experiences?

10. Why was education so important to Mercy? How does she show this in the book? What one event in the early chapters causes Mercy to look at education differently? What were the reasons for her to pursue an advanced degree later in life?

11. Why does the writer use poetry in the book?

12. How are Yankees portrayed in the book? Which examples are used to show how R.C., Mercy and others view them? How does the term *hillbilly* impact Mercy? Is this a term appreciated by other Appalachians? Why or why not?

13. Explain why Mercy resents her position as a female growing up in the 1960s. What examples in the story show this resentment?

14. Why does Mercy decide to abandon her mother? How does she rationalize the decision to disengage? Do you agree or disagree with her decision? What did she expect to experience when she found her mother? Was Mercy's desire to locate her birth mother rooted in reality or fantasy?

15. What is the author's purpose of adding "Life Lessons" at the end of the book?

16. Explain the family's dysfunction in the early chapters vs. dysfunction in later chapters.

17. Why do you think the author used counseling techniques and terminology in the novel? Was it effective?

18. Why did Nell abandon her children? Was it justified? How does she appear to rationalize her decision? Or does she? Do you think she really loved her children?

19. Which characters in the early chapters appear to have experienced the most difficult time in life? Mercy? R.C.? Nell? Granny? Grandpaw? The other children? What events support your idea?

20. Compare and contrast Mercy's early homes vs. the house discussed in the chapter "Livin' in a Mansion." What is she most proud of in that home? Why?

21. What was the significance of Mother's Day, the gift of the Peace Lily and the statement, "I forgive you, Mother?"

22. Why do you think Nell left her children? How have societal views and social services, as well as other agencies that now help abused women, changed since Nell's time?

23. Explain the reasons Nell's sister and other family members hid her address from Mercy. What do you think of their reasoning? Were they justified in doing so?

www.ingramcontent.com/pod-product-compliance
Lightning Source LLC
Chambersburg PA
CBHW031125090426
42738CB00008B/980